Natural Born Conservative

Published in the United States by
No Tomorrow Publishing, LLC, Florida

ISBN 978-1548378769
Ebook ISBN **1548378763**

Cover Design by Steven Novak
http://www.novakillustration.com/- *he's great!*

Edited by Sandra Nguyen
A Fresh Set of Eyes Editing and Writing Services
https://www.facebook.com/SFreshSetofEyes/

Typeset in Garamond.

NATURAL BORN CONSERVATIVE

KIARA ASHANTI

DEDICATION

This book is dedicated to millions (yes millions) of out spoken black conservatives in the country who fight to push our community back to their roots. A dedication also goes out to their family and friends, who wonder why they are conservative and Republican. Here as some answers to that question.

Join us!

CONTENTS

INTRODUCTION

I get the question all the time, from all types of people. A look of disbelief and shock usually accompanies the query.

"You're a *Republican?* How can that *be?*"

"Be" is usually at a higher vocal octave, emphasizing the state of disbelief in the questioner. I have gotten this reaction for years, decades even, and it still amuses me. In fairness, I cannot blame the incredulity.

I'm a black man. My name, Kiara Ashanti, is an African name. I sport long dreadlocks as my hairstyle of choice. Whatever image a person may have in their head about how a black Republican would look, I do not fit the image.

But Republican I am. Republican I have been, or leaned, as long as I can remember. I have no shame in the designation. I wear the mantle proudly, and often loudly. I have never been in the political closet, so to speak.

I have—or had—always chalked up the surprise at my political affiliation to the natural consequence of neither whites nor blacks knowing any black Republicans. One person once told me that it was easier to find a gay person than a black Republican. Even though I knew that based on pure numbers, that was false, I still could not argue against the sentiment. Blacks are known for many things: being great at sports, singing, dancing, and being Democrats. Before

1

cable news and social media, the only black Republicans anyone might hear from or about in the public arena were Clarence Thomas, former Congressman Jesse Watts, Colin Powell, and Condi Rice.

I thought Facebook and Twitter had definitively changed that. I routinely saw posts from other blacks like myself—people who had rejected the cultural hegemony in black America to be dyed-in-the-wool Democrats. A post I made in 2012 changed all of that.

On April 28th, I did what millions of people worldwide do every day; I was checking my Facebook page. While reading the news feed of comments submitted by my Facebook connections, I noticed a striking picture in the instant news feed to the right. It was a picture of a black man, staring resolutely from the screen with the title, "You don't understand why I'm conservative." To the right of the black male were seven statements about why he was conservative. The words struck me instantly, because they were true, on point, and they summed up why I was conservative.

I decided to share the picture, but instead of just sharing it on my page, I went one step further. I saved the picture and uploaded it as my new timeline banner. I wanted the statement to be there for all to see when they came to my page.

I do that a lot in life. If something is worth saying, I say it loud, often, and strongly. If something is worth fighting for, then I fight hard. At the time, I did not think much of the post, beyond the idea that my Democratic friends were going to be shaking their heads at me. After posting the picture, I went to bed.

The next morning when I did a quick Facebook check, I had sixty-five new friend requests and ten private messages. All of them were in response to the picture. I accepted all the requests and went on with my day. Later that afternoon, and I had fifty-two more friend requests and twelve more private messages. I accepted all those as well. Later that evening I signed in again, and again I had more friend requests—this time seventy-two. By the end of the weekend, I had accepted 400 new friends to my Facebook account. By the end of the month, I had 1,245 new friends. The picture in question has been shared over 1,545 times and counting on Facebook. One of my new friends edited the picture, putting my photo in place of the other one. That photo has been shared over 10,000 times and has to date 25,000 comments on the thread.

I do not know why the picture went on a mini-viral roll. I did not create the picture; I just shouted it from the mountain tops, so to speak, on my page. I can only imagine how many shares it got from the original poster. I do know this, though—the messages resonated in a deep fashion with conservatives. It touched them on an emotional, visceral level. More important, every message I got was either one of admiration or questions about how other blacks react to my conservatism. Most felt the need for more information from me.

Why was I conservative? How could I be conservative? How could *any black person* be conservative?

This book is the answer; at least in part. Every black Republican has their own story or reasons for turning away from the Democratic Party. Nonetheless, we have commonalities in our experience and reasoning. The huge response to this photo, and the questions that followed in its mini viral wake, tells me that people are desperate to understand.

Natural Born Conservative is my story about why I chose the Grand Ole Party, and I will provide insights into why public figures like Herman Cain, Condi Rice, Dr. Ben Carson, and others chose Conservatism as well. It will expand on the seven tenets expounded in the photo that serve as the catalyst for me writing this book.

In the end, you will know the path that leads me to conservatism, and you will know why millions of blacks and whites together have joined our path as well.

CHAPTER ONE
No, I Don't Hate Myself

The questions are common, repeated, and sometimes tedious. When asked--and it always is--the questions usually sound like the following:

"Why are you a Republican?"

"I cannot believe you are a Republican!"

"How could you possibly be a Republican?"

"Are you serious? Come on, you're joking."

"Why would you want to support *those* people?"

"Are you black?"

"I think you just say that because you want to be different or outside the box."

And my personal favorite, uttered to me in complete sincerity by no fewer than four women:

"I cannot believe I'm dating a Republican!"

In nearly all my interactions with fellow African-Americans, if I do not know the people, then I expect the question at some point. What follows is a conversation in which I try to explain why I am a Republican and do not support Democrats. The person to whom I am usually speaking gives what I'm saying as much attention as they do the wind blowing through tree leaves. Instead of listening, they spend their energy trying to show me why I'm wrong. They want to enlighten me as to why I need to have a 'come to Jesus' moment. If I do not, then usually I'm accused of hating myself. Though sometimes, they just give me a look of disgust, like they have just stepped on something unpleasant.

Conventional wisdom says that if you are born black; along with having a perfect, permanent tan, the word Democrat is stamped on your forehead. Being black and being a Democrat is as much a given as Italians and Lasagna—except the lasagna makes more sense. But I'm getting ahead of myself. The point is I'm supposed to love Democrats because I'm black.

This is the view of my community, so it is not surprising to me that white people are shocked when they meet someone black, who is a Republican or conservative. Before Facebook, the number of black conservatives I knew was a grand total of one, me! Social media has opened the world to everyone to find others of like minds, in all types of groups. Still, in the day-to-day life, a black conservative is a rarity.

The inspiration for this book is not so much the reaction to the values stated in the picture I posted on Facebook, but more to the genuine surprise, delight, and happiness expressed in all the private messages sent to me. The people who sent me messages all wanted to know how I escaped having the Democrat brand seared into my soul. The goal in this book, as stated in my introduction, is to give my reasoning and explain why the real puzzle should be—Why aren't all blacks Republican? But first, let me explain upfront what the reasons are not.

I WAS NOT BORN RICH

I always find it odd that Republicanism is associated with being rich when there are plenty of rich liberals. Many of the most liberal people around (someone say Hollywood!) are also some of the wealthiest people in the country. Wealth, at least on the surface, has nothing to do with why anyone is Republican, least of all myself. My mother did not raise me with a silver spoon, as the saying goes. I grew up just like millions of other Americans across the country, as a middle-class child. And when I say middle-class, I mean lifestyle, not income.

My father was in the Air Force, but died early in my life. That left my mother alone to raise my younger brother and me. Thanks to the service my father provided this country, my mother could raise my brother and me with his military benefits. The benefits we had were not the type you get after retiring from Goldman Sachs. We had a modest income, but she could not spend money willy-nilly. Lucky for me, my mother was a sharp, intelligent woman who was good at budgeting.

As a result, I lived a stereotypical American life. We had a house, a car, and a television. We lived in the suburbs, and I had clean clothes. If you asked me when I was eight years old, "are you rich?" I would have looked at you like you had lost your damned mind. I didn't know how much money my mother had, but I knew I did not get everything I wanted. I heard the words, "that is too expensive," more than once from mommy dearest. I knew we were not rich, but I never had to worry about food. The only time I went to bed hungry was when I did something I was not supposed to do.

Does that make me luckier than many people in the country? Yes, it does. Does that mean I lived some privileged life that accounts for my belief in conservative principles? Not directly, no. There are a whole lot of blacks who grew up more privileged than I, income wise, who did not turn onto the righteous path of conservatism. Yes, I did say righteous, but more on that later.

Although I lived in the 'burbs, I spent time in what most people would consider the ghetto; or inner city as we are calling it these days. My mother had six other siblings, and I spent a great deal of time at the homes of my aunts and grandparents on my mother's side. They all lived in Camden, New Jersey. If you have never heard of Camden, just know that this city is always in competition with Detroit as one of the worst inner-city areas in the country. The murder rate is high, drug use astronomical, and most people living in Camden are receiving some sort of governmental assistance. That's how it is today. It was not as bad when I was a child, but it was still bad enough that if you could afford not to live in Camden, you damned well did not.

My aunts would have been considered working class. They had jobs, and at times when they did not have or could not find work, I know some of them would accept welfare for a short time. Emphasis on 'short time.' They used it the way it was designed to be used—as a safety net, not as some unending governmental allowance.

Why does this matter? The reason is because I spent at least half my time as a child running around the streets of Camden with my cousins, and sleeping at their house or apartment. The inner city, and the problems of those who live there, are not foreign to me. As I have said, I have never had to worry about food, but when my mother called me in for lunch, she was not serving me caviar. When I was at my aunt's house, and she called us in for lunch, it was often a grilled cheese sandwich made from that large block of government cheese. I have drunk milk, both at my aunts and my own house made from powdered instant milk. Long before food stamps turned into EBT cards, I remember my aunt giving me a book of actual stamps, worth different amounts of money, to go to the corner store to buy eggs, juice, or more of that cursed powdered milk.

I had no silver spoon. If I had anything silver at all, it was the silver lining of having a father who had served this country long enough for our family to have retirement benefits when he died. That retirement, and my mother's proper stewardship of it, allowed her to be at home when I got home from school, and drag her all over town for my soccer, BMX racing, or whatever other craziness I was into as a young boy.

With the obvious exception of growing up without a father, I lived the American apple-pie childhood—middle-class, the term every Democrat President proclaims he is fighting to increase. That was my family. I was better off than some, but not as lucky, wealth-wise, as quite a few other Americans. Neither the money we did have, nor the money we did not, had anything to do with why I turned out as a Republican.

I'M NOT A CARBON COPY OF MY PARENTS BELIEFS

There is a strange phenomenon within family dynamics. Children often spend their teenage and young adult lives desperate not to be their parents. It is more than just rebellion. There is an almost instinctive need to be the exact opposite of how your father or mother was. However, studies have shown that the easiest way to have a general idea of what someone will believe as an adult is by looking at the values of the parents. Yes, this is not always the case. In the 60s, there were many white Americans who rebelled against the prejudices and racist ideas that some of their parents held. Still, many kids wake up one day, discover they are adults, and much to their eternal horror, discover they have become their mom or dad. The two areas this happens most in are religion and politics.

In my house, growing up, I had no clue whether my mother was a Democrat or Republican. I do not even remember her telling me she was going to go vote. I never overheard her talking about politics or social problems. I never saw a political book lying around the house, which is strange, because there were books all over our house. Maybe most importantly, my mother and I never talked about politics; at least not as a child. Once I had graduated from college, there were talks, but not between the ages of conception and twenty-four.

Instinctively, I know this is odd. I know that even if parents do not directly talk to their kids about politics, kids are usually bound to hear them saying something to a family member, a neighbor, or to the television set that would reveal how they feel. None of that happened to me growing up. Maybe it is because I would have rolled my eyes and said, "Um… yeah sure mom, Democrat… right, got it, and can I go play now?" I had very little patience for being in the house for anything other than food, television, or reading a book. Even when it came time for the 'birds and the bees' conversation, I wanted no part of it. I wanted to ride my bike and climb a tree.

If you do not talk about something, that leaves it up to you to discover your opinion on your own. That can be good or bad. In my case, it was glorious, because it allowed me to form an opinion based on the values my mother did spend time trying to impart to me, and not spitting out some default belief, like a robot.

Discussing or hearing your parents demonize one side or the other is not the only path to inserting influence on which political side a kid takes; not so if you are an African-American. As a black person in America, you must deal with social issues on a whole other level. If you are black, then the issue of race, as it was when I was growing up, is a true issue. Ideas around racism, prejudice, black identity, and many others are subjects necessary for a black parent to discuss with their kids. How they do that often determines, to some degree, how they will view whites, racism, and the opportunities they have in this country.

For my part, up until my third high school (we moved a lot), most of the cities we lived in were predominantly white. I have attended a school where I was the only black person in the school. I have lived in a neighborhood where there was only one other black family. I have been called a nigger. Yes, I did write the word out. We shall dispense with this politically correct "N-word" nonsense. If the word nigger makes you uncomfortable, good—it's supposed to. It is an ugly word with an ugly history. Eighty percent of the white friends and people I encountered growing up as a young boy never called me that. Twenty percent of them did, and I punched all those people in the face. Problem solved, as far as I was concerned.

Nonetheless, race and racism is not something my mother discussed at length with me. Why that is, I have no idea. I can only speculate, but there is one conversation I remember crystal clear. It was about the idea, and often the fact at that time, that blacks had to work twice as hard as whites to get the same level of credit for something. We had to be the best. We had to be excellent if we wanted to be noticed, get that raise, get on the team, etc. I do not remember how the conversation started, but I remember how my mother ended it.

"Yes, it is true that in this country you have to be twice as good as the white person. You have to be excellent, where they can be just okay. So what! That's right, so what. You're supposed to be excellent anyway. You're supposed to work at being the best on the team anyway. It doesn't matter if the whole team is black. You are supposed to try still to be better than everyone on the team. In school, you should be trying to get A's, not to be even with the white kids, but because you're supposed to get A's. I got A's in school. I was valedictorian, and not to prove I was as good as the white kids. I did it because I wanted to learn, and I wanted a better life. Forget about being seen as good as they are, be seen as better than they are, and BE better than everyone else is, black or white."

Those are the words my mother spoke to me about racism. I can truly say it is one of the seminal moments and conversations I had with my mother. I might have never lived up to that expectation, but I tell you there are few things in my life I remember better than that conversation right there.

IT'S NOT BECAUSE I'M MORALLY PERFECT

In the public space, conservatives and Republicans represent ourselves as the party of values. "Family values" is the moniker the mainstream media uses to encompass all the values that Republicans believe in and fight to uphold: values regarding morals, the protection of life, religious faith, and the sanctity of marriage. That is what we talk about and believe.

This creates a problem.

That problem is that as human beings, not everyone follows through on values of any kind. People—liberals and conservatives alike—lie, cheat, pander, make corrupt decisions, and make mistakes. Because Republicans are the party of values, when a Republican falls off the wagon, so to speak, it is a much bigger deal than if a Democrat does. There is nothing in the media better than a prominent Republican going through a sex scandal or accused sex scandal. President Donald Trump was roasted in the media about comments he made to entertainment reporter, Billy Bush, about grabbing women. Democrats were shocked and appalled. Meanwhile, old Billy Clinton essentially used his position of power to have sexual relations in the Oval Office, but that was just "sex" at the time. This is a clear hypocrisy on the part of the media and Democrats, *but*, to be fair, if you're going to call yourself the party of family values, then you set the bar higher for yourself. Our rhetoric makes Democrats believe that conservatives consider themselves better, more moral, and more righteous than other people.

This is somewhat true. If you wish to kill—oh, I'm sorry—I meant to say 'make a health care choice' regarding a baby because you did not use birth control when you hooked up with the cute guy or gal in the accounting department, I feel confident saying I'm better than you for wanting to see that baby live. Conservatives believe that judgments should be made on your behavior and mine. There are definitive right and wrong. That does not mean, however, that we are incapable of making decisions that can and should be considered wrong.

I am not perfect. If I were perfect, I would be a billionaire, married to the perfect wife with supermodel looks, and have perfect kids. I have none of those things. I have made mistakes in my life. I have made decisions in the past that do not hold up to conservative standards. I am no different from anyone else.

One of the most sacred values a conservative has is that of protecting innocent life. There is maybe no other issue that separates Republicans from Democrats clearer than that of abortion. As a young man in college, my attitude was like most young people, I think. If a woman wanted an abortion and it was in the first three months, I did not have a problem with it. In my mind, it was not really a baby yet.

For people who have always been pro-life, that sounds completely ridiculous. They are correct. Scientifically, it's a human life. It's not as if the DNA is that of a cat, which transforms into a human later. As I tell my friends now, what do you think will happen to that mass of dividing cells? Do you think it will turn into a tire, a toaster, a little puppy dog? No, it will become a baby, because it is a baby. At age 21, I did not think like that, though. I was more concerned with my future. I was concerned about the cost of a baby. I saw it as an obstacle to all the goals I was working toward in college.

At that young age, it never occurred to me that a decision to have unprotected sex was the real obstacle to any goals I had. I never thought, "Hey, even if I use a condom, she could still get pregnant, and her getting pregnant and thus ruining (because in my mind, everything would be ruined) my goals was my fault. None of this occurred to me, because as a young and immature kid, I was consumed with self-absorption. It was all about me and my life. In short, I was selfish. The world revolved around little ol' me. But a funny thing happened to me.

I grew the hell up.

I now understand the world revolves around the sun, and I'm neither the sun nor the moon. I learned that my decisions are the issue, not an innocent baby. If I do not want to be a father, I have options:

- Do not have sex.
- Use a condom.
- Make sure my partner is on birth control.

There are some Democrats who have matured in this fashion. Unfortunately, most of them are not elected Democrats in the Congress and Senate. I think it is fair to say the majority of the Democrat voting public are pro-choice and insist on thinking of babies as something that is not a consequence of their own choices. Luckily, I have never had that situation.

That does not mean, however, that I am incapable of making that or any number of other mistakes. If this or any book of mine becomes a runaway bestseller, you can bet your life someone is going to try and investigate me, try to find some dirt or a less-than-flattering historical nugget. They will use this as ammunition to say, "*See, he doesn't even follow his own beliefs. He's a fraud.*" Well, I'm not. If I do something wrong, that does not make it okay. Newt Gingrich cheated on two wives; you can attack him on that, but that does not mean adultery is okay.

I did not choose conservatism because I woke up one day and said, "I'm better than these Democrats, and I can do no wrong." I daresay, no person becomes a conservative because of thinking like that. Whether it is by moral, financial, or social issues, I have made mistakes. I learn from my mistakes—or try to, at least. I try to do better. That is what makes me human, but it is not why I am conservative.

I'M NOT SELFISH

This is maybe the most irritating opinion of Democrats--especially black Democrats.

"*Republicans are selfish and greedy.*"

"*They do not care about anyone else.*"

"*All they care about is making a buck, and they will step on you in order to do it.*"

I hear this all the time, and let me tell you, if you are a Democrat reading this and you believe that, then you are a complete sanctimonious ass.

There have been numerous studies and surveys in the private sector, in books like "Who Really Gives," by Arthur C. Brooks, and at universities that show self-described conservatives give more to charity than Democrats. Conservatives give two-thirds more in financial donations to charity. You could say, "*it's easier for fat-cat Republicans to give more, they have more money.*" Sorry, but as we used to say in the 80s, "not todaaay." Conservatives at all income levels give more than Democrats. A conservative who makes $50,000 a year gives more than a Democrat who makes $50,000 a year. Of course, financial giving is not the only form of charity. How about this, conservatives donate more blood annually than Democrats do. Or, how about time? I had a friend that was positively addicted to volunteerism. It was her drug of choice, but even with her holding the bag for her team, conservatives still donate more time to charities than do Democrats[12].

Does this somehow diminish the time, money, and blood that Democrats do give to charity? No, it does not. As a conservative, I would not make that assertion. Charity is a great thing to do, no matter who does it. But this notion that Democrats have some sort of moral lock and monopoly on caring for others is nonsense.

1 http://www.realclearpolitics.com/articles/2008/03/conservatives_more_liberal_giv.html
2 https://www.amazon.com/Who-Really-Cares-Compassionate-Conservatism/dp/0465008232

I do not volunteer often, but I give to charity. I learned to at an early age. Growing up, when I got my first paper route, my mother told me, "*You save 10%, and you give 10% to the church or charity.*" She sometimes slacked on making me save the 10%, but she made darn sure the 10% to the church got put in the collection plate, every time.

I am not a selfish man. I was raised better than that. I give to my friends; I give to charity. I believe people need help sometimes, and they should get that help. If at some point, I find myself super rich, then I know I should give money to charity. It is the right thing to do, and I'm not going to heaven with my mother pissed off at me for not doing it.

NO, I DO NOT HATE MYSELF

"*I don't care what you say, Kiara. He (President Obama) got Bin Laden. And I still say you do not like yourself. You hate being black.*"

Those are the words of—wait for it—a friend. Yes, I know, "With friends like that, who needs enemies?" She has said the same sentiment many different times. Here is another one—"*God, Kiara, sometimes I wonder about you. It's like you have self-hatred or something. You are black, you know.*"

This one was from a Facebook friend in response to a comment I made about the ridiculousness of some blacks not having a photo ID. I basically asserted that if you weren't willing to go and get an ID from the DMV, you were either lazy or irresponsible. I figure, hey, if you have no problem showing ID to drink at a bar, then surely you can get one to vote. I mean, it's not as if you must fight through a horde of dogs, the KKK, or fire hoses to get one at the DMV.

There are few things that piss me off more than being told I hate myself because I am not a Democrat. It is the one string of words that can bring me to the brink of grabbing someone by the neck and throttling them. I have been on the cusp, very often, of cursing a friend out in a way that would end the relationship in an instant. However, if you are black and you do not support Democrats, Al Sharpton, Jesse Jackson, and any social problem that blacks have jumped on the bandwagon about, then you do not like your blackness. You are in fact, an Uncle Tom.

In the black community, you cannot critique, criticize, or bad mouth a single thing the African-American community at large does. If you do, then you hate yourself. That is unless you are white, then if you do any of those things, you are a racist and hate black people.

Well, surprise, surprise, but I do not hate myself. I do not look in the mirror and wish I was white. I do not try to "act white." Most of the people I interact with on a personal basis are black. I'm not putting on a show for anyone.

Truth be told, my blackness is no different from a person's whiteness. It is a simple fact of birth. It is no more deserving of default love or affection than being born a man or woman. Having black skin does not convey any special powers on me or inure me with any sort of inherent evil powers. Simply put, anyone who loves themselves just because they are black, white, Asian, or whatever is suffering from delusion. Blacks have no problem telling a white person, "You ain't special just because you are white." Well, guess what? Being black does not make us special either.

I have no reason to hate myself. I'm a good person who helps my friends without a second thought. I'm the type of person who whether you are a friend or a passing associate, if I run across information or tools that might help in your goals, I pass along that information. I respect myself because no matter the place, person, or occasion, I will stand up for the correct values. I do not waver; I do not shrink from it, just because of fear about how others will perceive me. I love myself, and see myself as a worthy person because I have character, and that has nothing to do with my skin color.

My mother did not raise me to be a Democrat or Republican. She raised me to be a good person who believes in fairness, hard work, and treating people well who deserve it. I learned most of those lessons well. If she were alive today, I imagine I would have the following conversation with her:

Kiara: Mom, some of my friends do not think I like myself because I am conservative. They think I'm practicing self-hate because I vote Republican.

My mother: What does being a Democrat or Republican have to do with your skin color? What does liking or not liking yourself have to do with the color of your skin? Are they saying you would love yourself more if you were white? I wasn't aware that all white people were Republicans.

Her response would be derision toward the people saying these things to me, because the basis by which they are making the determination is utterly stupid.

I do not hate being black. I do not see my blackness as something to inherently love or hate. Sure, there are real-life cultural things unique to African-Americans in this country. I know what they are, I tease my white friends about them, and I know I really did not have anything to do with their creation. So I do not feel the need to somehow, on a deeper level, believe these cultural things make me special as a black man. Do you really think black soul singers sing better because of the color of their skin? Hell, if a white person spends enough time in the tanning salon, they will look black. They may look a little strange, but they can get just as dark as some of us blacks. When they do, do you think they are going to burst into song and sound like Whitney Houston? Are they going to start dancing like Michael Jackson?

I'm snippy because my friends and those in the media who accuse black conservatives of "self-hate" are being stupid. They are also ignorant of their own history. Dr. Martin Luther King was a conservative and registered Republican, as was his father. Medgar

Evers was a conservative. These two men lost their lives fighting for blacks; did they have self-hatred as well? Harriet Tubman was a Republican, as were half the founding members of the NAACP. Did they hate being black?

Not a single black person was born with "Democrat" stamped on their forehead. I look at the policies of the Democrats, and the results they have produced within the black community—which is to say, the lack of results, and I quite intelligently walk away. The idea that millions of African-Americans have not done the same thing is more closely related to self-loathing than being a Republican.

And that's the rub of it. At the end of the day, blacks believe you need to support Democrats because they support blacks. Democrats work for policies that help the black community. Democrats feel our pain and wish to end it. Democrats like and love blacks.

Except they do not.

Their policies, as you will learn in coming chapters, do not work. Their social agenda is antithetical to everything that is taught in the black church and being a Christian. Their foundation is one that has opposed black freedom and civil rights for most of this great country's history. Hell, even the term "black Republican" does not mean what people think.

That term does not originate as a description of Herman Cain or me. It was a term of derision created by the Democrat party to describe whites who were fighting to end slavery. That is the party that blacks are fighting for in the public discourse. With a history like that, how can anyone say I'm the one with self-hatred? No, no, no, if that disease is going around, then it's the blacks who support Democrats who have both the disease and are the carriers.

Let me make this plain. I am not a Republican because I hate black people. I am a Republican because I hate what Democrat policies have done to black people.

The reason I have taken the time and effort to list these things is because they are the reasons I hear most often from people who question why I would be a conservative. They are smoke screens and nothing else. Democrats use these things as ways to distract from real issues. It is easier to view me as an Uncle Tom, instead of looking at the facts regarding African-American life under Democratic and liberal policies. It is easier to talk about a phony war on women, instead of being confronted by your own irresponsible behavior regarding sex. All these excuses are used not to have to deal with facts or truth. It is what people do when they do not want to deal with the truth. That's rule one in Sal Alinsky's Rules for Radicals. Attack the person. Notice not one of the things I listed have anything to do with issues. They are all indictments on me as a person, not on ideas. That is because when it comes to ideas, particularly as they pertain to African-Americans, Democrats lose that game.

I shall show you in excruciating detail just how much Democrats have screwed over the black community. I promise that by the end of this book; you will know why I choose the Right side of things. More important, I will do this not based on my opinion. There will be no wild, unfounded assertions. I can and will do this based on facts that anyone can find in reputable texts and websites.

Black Democrats, black liberals, and black power enthusiasts love to quote a 1970s saying as a rallying cry, "I'm black and I'm proud." I say two things. One, good for you. Glad to hear it. Second, here is my rallying cry, my call to arms,

"I'm black, conservative, and proud!"

CHAPTER TWO
The KKK, Jim Crow, and the
Architects of American Racism

"...now you have the Republicans, who want to literally drag us all the way back to Jim Crow laws..."
- Debbie Wasserman,
Chair of the Democratic National Committee

"The tea party people are kind of, like—without robes and hoods, they have really shown a very hard-core, angry side of America that is against any type of diversity. And we saw opposition to African-Americans, hostility toward gays, hostility to anybody who wasn't just, you know, a clone of George Wallace's fan club."
- Congressman Steve Cohen, TN

"I'm a student of it, as well, of the tea party crowd. Who are these people? How much of it is racial? How much of it is ideological? How much of it is rooted in organizations like, well, the Know-Nothings, the KKK, et cetera?"
- Chris Matthews, MSNBC

These seem to be appeals to the extreme white wing of the Republican Party. That is to say that there continues to be among many conservatives a real resentment against blacks.... I think this is very intentional, it is pandering, there's sort of a wink-wink that this base should be reminded that Barack Obama, President of the United States, is one of them, an African-American. Yes, I think this is very intentional. I think it is part of a hateful campaign that is being very methodically run in the hope it's going to appeal to voters who would love to see us return to the good old days of Jim Crow.'

– Former CNN correspondent Bob Franken talking about the GOP candidates on MSNBC's Politics Nation, January 6.

"We are going to take on the barbarism of war, the decadence of racism, and the scourge of poverty, that the Ku Klux -- I meant to say the Tea Party..."

-Rev. Walter E. Fauntroy

History is more than a collection of events that have happened in the past. It is a textbook, a guidepost, and a map of human decisions, actions, and viewpoints. It can also be society's most enduring form of cultural rebuke. Society and institutions change, but when the past does not align with the current state of values, often a country is stuck fighting that past.

The Germans are still under the shadow of Hitler's evil in many ways. Political and social policy in Germany is affected by the Nazis' past. Modern Germans want to stay away from the stigma of Nazism the way a germophobe stays away from garbage.

America is no different. Our cultural mythos as a nation of freedom has a dent in its shiny bell. Slavery, followed by Jim Crow, is our great sin. It's a sin that haunts the country to this day. No one wants to be associated with the racist viewpoints of the past in America, to the point that merely making the accusation is still a potent weapon.

American politicians, as those quotes above show, throw the past around like throwing knives. The best way in the mind of a Democrat to mobilize blacks and "good whites" against their opponents, usually Republicans, is to invoke the racism of the past. It is effective. It is also disingenuous.

When talking about the racism of the past, especially when people bring it up as a reason I should run away from Republicans, I find it best to look at timelines. That is right, timelines. If a photograph is worth a thousand words, then a timeline chart is at least worth five hundred words. See, a timeline gives you a visual picture of the truth. It shows patterns in a clearer manner than words could ever do. Here is a timeline of America, vis-a-vis the political parties.

Let me break this down for you in detail:

1775- The slave trade starts.

1854- The Whig party, which would become the Republican Party, is formed as an anti-slavery movement.

1860- The term "black Republican" is coined as a slur for abolitionist forces by the Democratic presidential candidate, James Holcombe.

1861- Republican President Abraham Lincoln declares Civil War over the issue of ending slavery*.

1863- President Lincoln issues the Emancipation Proclamation, ending slavery.

1866- The Ku Klux Klan is formed—by southern Democrats.

1866- Jim Crow law of separate-but-equal status is formulated.

1875- Republicans Charles Sumner and Benjamin Butler pass the Civil Rights Act of 1875, outlawing Jim Crow. Democrats fought it.

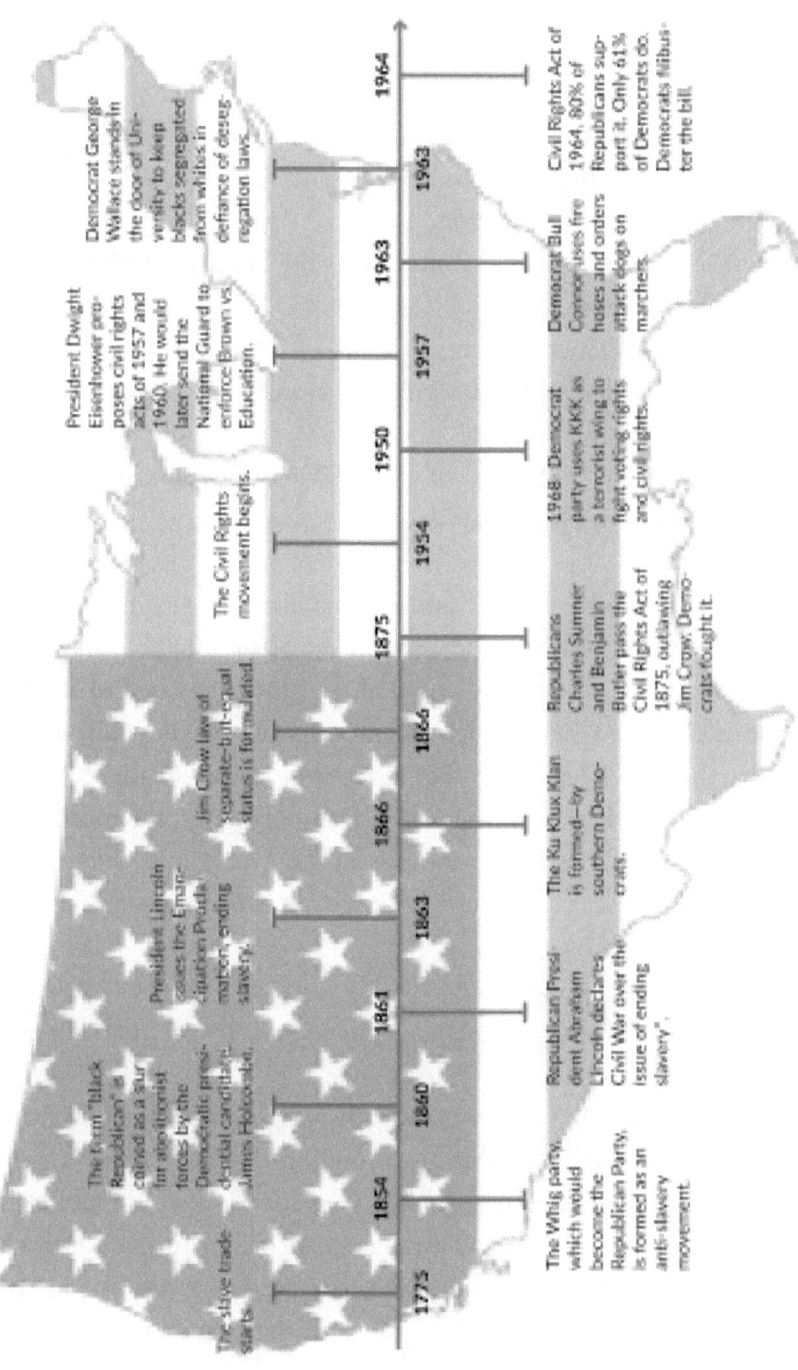

1954- The Civil Rights movement begins.

1950-1968- Democrat party uses KKK as a terrorist wing to fight voting rights and civil rights.

1957- President Dwight Eisenhower proposes civil rights acts of 1957 and 1960. He would later send the National Guard to enforce Brown vs. Education.

1963- Democrat Bull Connor uses fire hoses and orders attack dogs on marchers.

1963- Democrat George Wallace stands in the door of University to keep blacks segregated from whites in defiance of desegregation laws.

1964- Civil Rights Act of 1964. 80% of Republicans support it. Only 61% of Democrats do. Democrats filibuster the bill.

What this chart shows, and it's a small one, is that throughout the turbulent history of racism in America, Republicans have fought against it. The very origin of the party was as a anti-slavery movement. So when modern Democrats call out the pain of the past, they are lying when they place that history at the doors of Republicans. Bull Connor was a Democrat, not a Republican. Without the force of Republicans in the House and Senate, the Civil Rights Act would have never made it to Johnson's desk. It was being blocked.

Whenever confronted by these inconvenient historical nuggets, black and white Democrats retreat to the same defense: the Southern Strategy.

The Southern Strategy is the idea that Richard Nixon went to the south to recruit disillusioned southern Democrats, who were racist, into the Republican Party. The idea is that Republicans appealed to racism and racists views of blacks to get southern white votes. Once that happened, the parties transformed. The Democrats "became Republicans," and the Republicans became "the Democrats." The parties did a body switch. The Democrats were now tolerant and anti-racism, while the Republicans retained their racist roots from when they used to be Democrats. If that sounds confusing, it is because it *is* twisted and confusing. The bottom line is that this narrative seeks to assert that the Democrat party you see today is the same party that fought against slavery and Jim Crow; they just used to be called Republicans.

That is a convenient story, isn't it? Unfortunately, it is not true. The problem with the narrative is that if Democrats in the deep south moved to the Republican Party because of the Civil Rights Act, then deep southern states should have been the first states to move in that direction. However, the first states to trend Republican were North Carolina, Texas, Tennessee and Florida. The first people to move in these states were not poor angry whites. They were suburbanites. Also, it was clear to everyone that the Republicans had pushed for the passage of the Civil Rights Act. Why would you move toward a party over your hatred of civil rights, when that party is the one that got it passed? Lastly, when you look at the political and economic platforms of the Democrats then and now, they are the same. The political platform of the Democrats is why the suburbanites of the south moved into the Republican party. Democrats wanted higher taxes, were soft on defensive issues, and talked about a welfare state. They are the same policies Democrats push today.

Unfortunately, the arbiter of history for the masses is the national press. Calling the mainstream media (MSM) overwhelmingly liberal is not a conspiracy. I have been a freelance reporter and journalist for over ten years; I can tell you the accusation by conservatives on this point is true. The MSM love the narrative that says Democrats and liberals love black people, and that their political affiliation of choice has always been for equality. They have no incentive to oppose the myth. They are talking about themselves, after all, and who wants to see himself or herself as a bad person?

The teachers of history in both high school and college have the same problem. Most college professors are not just liberal, but often radical. They look in the mirror and want to believe their own myth about their party. It almost seems as if high schools barely teach American history any longer, let alone the detailed facts of the roots of America's political parties. Therefore, the Southern Strategy is one that is factual to them mentally, and in the way it is presented. Fortunately, we can still see the "D" after all the names of the politicians who were roadblocks to racial equality and civil rights. The history is there for us to see, if we are willing to look.

How did I find out the truth? I again thank my mother. You see, while she did not engage in political or social science-talk with me, she did impart one major lesson. That lesson was to question *everything*. Do not take anyone's word for anything. If a person is making an assertion, make them prove it. She did not care whether it was a teacher, cop, minister, or even herself. *"QUESTION EVERYTHING,"* were her words to me.

In college, when I was forced to take a liberal studies class, I found it odd that the Democrats of today were different from the Democrats of yesteryear when the tax policies were the same. How could that be? Shouldn't they be different? When my professor literally started stammering at the question, I knew there was a rat in the classroom. I could have left it there, but I did the research instead. I found out the truth and became the bane of that professor's existence.

Accusing Republicans of racism is part of nearly every Democrat's DNA. They cannot help themselves, especially since many are not taught history or politics in a neutral fashion. It helps their party stay in power in many areas of the country, especially the inner cities. Racism, or rather its accusation, has turned into a fine art.

Since the election of the first black President in the country's history, the rhetoric has risen to an unheard-of level. If you so much as say you do not like the tie President Obama is wearing, then you are a racist. In my book, Commander-in-Failure, I detail how America seemed hopeful for a post-racial America, but got race used as cudgel instead.

The reality of the past is that America overall was a racist nation that had people who chose to fight it. They did not believe in slavery. They did not believe blacks were inferior. The number of people who felt that way grew. As they grew in numbers, they gravitated toward clubs, organizations, and people who felt the same way. The Republican Party was one of those groups, filled with people of like mind.

So, what about today? If Republicans are not racist historically, and the Democrat party historically was, does that mean Democrats are racist today? The answer's obviously no.

Today's rank-and-file Democrat, sitting next to you in the coffee shop, does not hate black people. They do not want slaves; they do not want Jim Crow laws back. Today's Democrat is just ignorant of their party's history, and the effect of its policies on blacks, which we will delve into shortly.

The point of this chapter is that liberals cannot speak to me about the racist past of the Republican Party. All the racist events, beliefs, and laws they point to were either created by Democrats or were fought to be kept in place by Democrats. As the first line in the meme that serves as the inspiration for the writing of this book says, "I've read history and knew the KKK, and Jim Crow were supported by Democrats." You cannot place that on Republicans, or use it as a talking point to get me and other black Republicans to rethink our political choice.

Black and white Democrats alike like to paint the Democratic Party as the knights in shining armor for blacks. Unfortunately, and historically, those are just white sheets reflecting in the sun.

CHAPTER THREE
Black Genocide

When I was in college, I ran afoul of the student group the Black Student Union. As the name implies, it is a club specifically for blacks in predominantly white colleges. Ostensibly it is a club that has its roots in providing a common place for black students to meet each other. It also looks out for the concerns and issues that may have a specific impact on black students. An example would be that at one point, the African studies department at my alma mater, University of South Florida (USF), was going to be eliminated. The BSU fought to keep that department alive and funded.

However, like the Black Lives Matter movement of today, the BSU was often a breeding ground for Black Nationalist thinking. If we were in the 60's, it is where you would find all the black panthers congregating. I was never one for walking around with my fist held high with a black glove on it, literally or figuratively. I had a pro-American viewpoint, which is why I say I ran afoul of the club more than once with my pro-American and 'let's move on from the Civil Rights era' articles in the school newspaper.

Whenever I would get into debates with these people, either at the club meetings or around the campus, someone would always bring up a line that went something like this; "*Do you know how many liquor stores are in the hood? Why so many? You don't see a liquor store on every corner of white neighborhoods?"*

I never really understood the logic behind the statement, but I got the gist behind the question—especially when followed by a remark about drugs in the hood. The implication was clear. Liquor stores and/or drugs were allowed in high quantity in black communities by the government in order to impact the community-at-large negatively.

I always found this reasoning to be curious. Putting the truth or veracity of the belief aside, if you want to complain about businesses that negatively impact black communities, you must talk about Planned Parenthood. You should talk about the large number of clinics that provide abortions to pregnant black women. It does not matter if you think abortion should be legal. There certainly are not abortion clinics in white neighborhoods at the number or same level as there are in the black inner cities of America. If you want to discuss the negative impact, how about the impact of 15.1 million black babies aborted since 1973?

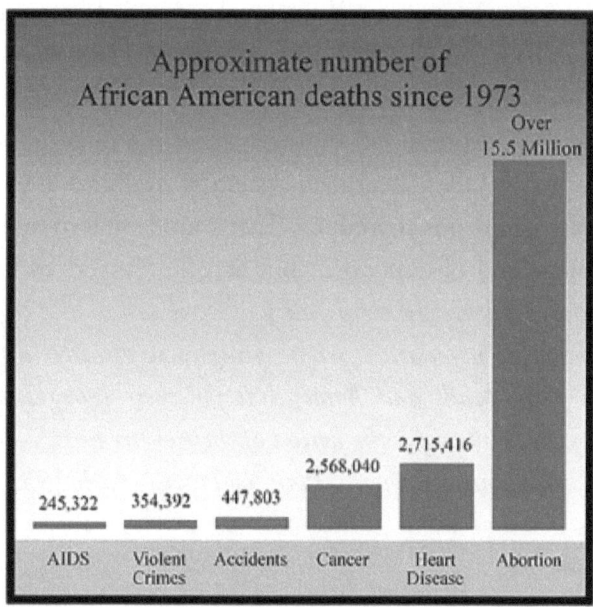

All figures are based on cumulative statistics provided
by the U.S. Center for Disease Control National
Vital Statistics Reports

There are 46 million blacks in the United States, as determined by the 2015 U.S. Census[3]. That means nearly half of the U.S. black population has been killed before they were ever born. By any definition that is genocide.

There is no group more synonymous with abortion than Planned Parenthood. They perform the most abortions, 323,999 in 2014-2015, as an organization. They also get more money from Congress as an abortion provider. In 2015, Planned Parenthood received $553.7 million of taxpayer money[4]. They claim that their funding is for needed healthcare services that help disadvantaged women, but not for abortions. Given that they have never had their accounting books examined, we can only take their word for it.

What is not up for dispute is that Democrats, especially black ones, defend Parenthood to the nth degree, which is a curious situation. Planned Parenthood not only terminates thousands of black pregnancies each year, but its founder, Margaret Sanger, was an avowed racist.

Margaret Sanger was a NY nurse who testified before the U.S. Senate in 1916 in support of Negative Eugenics. Negative Eugenics was the idea that the population needed to be controlled and the best way to do that was by segregating the undesirables from everyone else, and then creating a system of sterilization so that the undesirables could not reproduce. That sounds like something out of a dystopian end-of-days novel, but here are Sanger's own words:

"...apply a stern and rigid policy of sterilization and segregation to that grade of population whose progeny is already tainted...to apportion farm lands and homesteads for these segregated persons where they would be...for the period of their entire lives."– Margaret Sanger, Birth Control Review, "Plan for Peace," April 1932, Vol 26, Number 4

---

3 http://blackdemographics.com/population/
4 https://www.lifesitenews.com/news/planned-parenthood-performed-323999-abortions-and-received-553.7-million-fr

The words seem clear to me.

In 1921 Sanger founded the American Birth Control League, which later would become Planned Parenthood. She opened its facilities in predominantly black, immigrant, and poor neighborhoods. In 1939, Sanger began the aptly named Negro Project[5].

The Negro Project was an endeavor to get black women to use more birth control to decrease the population of blacks. She recruited black preachers to sermonize her message, the crux of which was the following:

Birth control itself often denounced as a violation of natural law, is nothing more or less than the facilitation of the process of weeding out the unfit, of preventing the birth of defectives or of those who will become defective." –Margaret Sanger, "Women and the New Race" Chapter 18

"We who advocate Birth Control, on the other hand, lay all our emphasis upon stopping not only the reproduction of the unfit but upon stopping all reproduction when there are not economic means of providing proper care..." –Margaret Sanger, "Birth Control and Racial Betterment" from Birth Control Review, Feb 1919, pg 11

The pattern that Sanger used, setting up shop in the black neighborhood and enlisting the help of the most trusted leaders in the community—preachers—is a pattern that holds to this day with Planned Parenthood. Their clinics are all over the inner cities. They enlist the help of black leaders, preachers, and black elected officials, to protect and promote their organization. The message about eugenics and the unfit is gone, but has been replaced with rhetoric about providing needed health care services for the poor.

For all the talk about Black Lives Matter and the rants by people like Jesse Jackson and Al Sharpton regarding police shootings of black people; more blacks have been killed in Planned Parenthood

5 "Birth Control and Racial Betterment", Birth Control Review, February 1919, pg 11, Margaret Sanger

clinics than by police officers. Go back and re-read the number. Fifteen million black fetuses have been aborted since 1973. These were babies who, if born, could have attended proms, high school graduations, birthday parties, and trips to the amusement park. They are real people who never got their chance, or their "choice," because black leaders in cahoots with Planned Parenthood have taught young black mothers that it is okay to kill your child.

Democrats like to bring up the KKK all the time with Republicans, even though Democrats founded them, but the founder of Planned Parenthood accepted the invitation to speak to several KKK groups. Just what could Sanger impart to the KKK that would have been good for blacks in America?

There is no doubt that access to birth control is a needed service; one that community health clinics could provide just fine. It is also true that a woman who has been raped or is the victim of incest should not be made to carry a baby to term. The woman is a victim in those situations. Her choice has been stolen from her. I have no use for men who do that to women and little girls. You could shoot them, hang them, or throw them off the side of a building for all I care.

However, by Planned Parenthood's own admission, the number of abortions due to rape is less than 1%[6]. There is a world of difference between deciding to have sex without a condom and getting pregnant, and being raped and becoming pregnant. In the latter, a woman's choice has been taken away. In the former, the woman has made a choice to have unprotected sex, and now wishes to take away a human life.

Regardless of a person's view on abortion, my beef is that historically, Planned Parenthood has taken more away from the black community than it has given to them. There were 337,000 abortions last year, equaling more lives taken away than those they saved.

What is also clear is that Democrats, in overwhelming numbers, fight for Planned Parenthood to be in those communities, while

6 http://abort73.com/abortion_facts/us_abortion_statistics

Republicans are fighting for thousands of black babies to remain alive in those communities. Black Democrats are fighting to preserve an organization that was founded based on hate, false science (Eugenics), and racism. Re-read those quotes and look for other ones if you must, but tell me how those statements cannot be construed as racist?

What is amusing is if you bring this up to any Democrat, assuming they know Sanger's history, they will immediately switch into a rant about what Planned Parenthood does today. The needed health services they provide, like mammograms? Oh wait, they don't provide mammograms.

I can hear the words from a Democrat or even Independent right now. *"Yes, they do. Planned Parenthood does provide mammograms!"* Oh, really? Here is an excerpt from Factcheck.org on this very issue, written after former President Barack Obama made this same claim.

> *"Women can't walk into a Planned Parenthood clinic and get a mammogram on the spot. The clinics don't have mammography equipment. Planned Parenthood performs gynecological exams, including breast exams, and refers women to other facilities to have mammograms performed, much like women are referred to radiological centers by their gynecologists or primary care physicians."*
>
> *In a statement sent to FactCheck.org, Dr. Deborah Nucatola, senior director of medical services for Planned Parenthood, said that "Planned Parenthood does help women nationwide get access to mammograms," as part of the health care services it provides to nearly 3 million persons each year[7].*

---

7 http://www.factcheck.org/2012/10/planned-parenthood-and-mammograms/

The quote from Nucatola reminds me of one those new commercials from LifeLock. The ones where they have a "cavity monitor." A guy goes to the dentist (he thinks) to fix a cavity in his tooth, and the non-dentist says, "Oh no, I'm not a dentist, I'm a cavity monitor. I just let you know if you have a cavity. You have a big one." Then the guy ducks out to lunch. He doesn't do anything about the cavity.

Planned Parenthood is a mammogram monitor. If you need one, they will refer you to a place to get one. But you cannot get it at their clinic. If, however, you go to a community health clinic, you can get a mammogram on premises. You can get something called pre-natal care as well. Can't do that at a Planned Parenthood clinic.

Planned Parenthood exists primarily to give abortions. That is their mission statement. It is how they make most of their money. To call it an abortion mill is not an understatement, but a factual description. And where are these mills located in high numbers? In black neighborhoods.

The black community makes up 13% of the population, but account for 37% of the abortions in America[8]. That's 3.7 times more often than for white women. I do not care what the race involved is—if you are killing half your population off, you cannot thrive.

Now, it would be fair to say, "*Hey, the economic conditions for blacks in the inner city are the reason more abortions happen. Go to the poor neighborhoods of whites and compare them to the white middle class, and you will see a big difference as well.*" That would be a correct point.

The problem is, whose fault is that? Democrats have overseen every inner city in America for the last five decades. If their policies uplift people, shouldn't we have seen the economic conditions of the inner city raised to the point where abortion is not a choice based on economics?

8 http://www.operationrescue.org/wp-content/uploads/2016/09/LifeDynamicsRacialReport.pdf

These are the questions that fly through my head. They are the questions I asked my professors in college, and they seldom had answers. Their attitude was one of "It's a woman's body, therefore everything else is moot." That would be at the start of the class, by the end of the class; they would be talking about how men have not "embraced their responsibility as fathers enough in modern times." In other words, a woman could skip on being a parent, but the man had no such moral option.

I could go over a hundred various reasons why abortion bugs me. I could recite the ways it negatively impacts the black community. But I don't have to do that. My biggest reason for hating this issue is in the eyes of every child I see. Kids are to be loved and protected. As adults, that is our moral and ethical obligation. All kids deserve to be born. For the most part, Republicans stand for that, and the Democrats who agree do not have high enough numbers to override the Democrats who do not believe all kids should be born. Therefore, I chose Republicans.

CHAPTER FOUR
Intellectual Dishonesty and
the Politics of Selective Outrage

There is one thing I cannot stand when it comes to debate or discussion on any topic, and that is hypocrisy and intellectual dishonesty. The kettle does not get to call the pot black in my world—*EVER*. If someone starts going down that route, then as Negan of Walking Dead fame says, "I will shut that shit down!" Hard.

In the rough-and-tumble of what we call modern day politics, I expect politicians to be hypocrites. The days of gentlemanly debate, and then compromise with a smile... if they ever existed, certainly do not exist now. Democrats (*read: Progressives*) and Republicans play to their bases and say what is necessary to support their team. They have no qualms about saying one thing today and saying something completely opposite tomorrow. Take for example the Biden Rule.

The Biden Rule is simple. In 1992 during an election year, then Senator Joe Biden said that President Bush should not nominate a Supreme Court Justice. The reasoning was simple, that the American people should have a say in the direction of the pick, vis-a-vis the election for the Presidency. Biden's words on the issue in 1992 were quite plain:

"It would be our pragmatic conclusion that once the political season is underway, and it is, action on a Supreme Court nomination must be put off until after the election campaign is over,"

- Senator Joe Biden, July 1992

1992 is a long time ago. Things change, correct? Well, in 2007 Senate Chuck Schumer said:

"We should not confirm any [George W.] Bush nominee to the Supreme Court, except in extraordinary circumstances."

- Senator Chuck Schumer, July 2007

That was said when the Presidential elections were nearly a year and a half away.

When Senate Republicans let it be known that Obama's nomination of Merrick Garland would not get a hearing in an election year and cited the Biden Rule, Democrats freaked. Schumer now said, *"There is no Biden Rule."* When one plucky reporter confronted the Senator about his former words, he made a squishy face, like he had just stepped on something unpleasant and walked away.

Still, he is a politician, and so I expect a certain level of boneheaded hypocrisy from him and others like him—Democrats and Republican alike. I do not give any leeway to pundits, commentators, or normal everyday people. If something bothers them, then I expect it to bother them regardless of who is doing it.

Nothing gets a Democrat hot and bothered more than the oppression or mistreatment of one of their protected groups. In years past, that protected group, or rather the group that needed someone to fight for them, was the so-called little guy—the person who did not have money, fancy lawyers, or political connections. Over the years, that has fallen by the wayside and shifted to a focus on identity politics. If you are an oppressed group, which in Democrat's eyes is anyone who is not a white male, then you need the Democrats to fight for you. They will champion your cause and fight your fight. To paraphrase Bill Clinton, "they feel your pain."

Unless, that is, you happen to be a Republican. Then your mistreatment is either okay, or coming right at the hands of the Democrats. There are numerous examples, but one of the best is Bill Clinton vs. Clarence Thomas.

In 1991, President Bush needed to fill the seat vacated by Thurgood Marshall. There was unprecedented pressure on Bush to nominate an African-American to the Court. If President Bush chose someone white, even if she was a woman, it would have been charged as a racially-motivated move in the eyes of Democrats and the mainstream press. They need not have been worried. Bush nominated a black man—one who got his law degree from Yale University Law School. But, of course, Bush had chosen a conservative-leaning judge.

Judge Thomas was qualified for the post, but his conservative bonafides meant he was unfit to serve in the eyes of blacks and Democrats. A full-court press was put on to derail his nomination, the center of which was Anita Hill.

Hill accused Thomas of sexually harassing her when they both worked at the Equal Opportunity Commission (EEOC). She never filed a complaint, an ongoing habit with accusations of this sort, I might add, and even followed Thomas—as her boss—to another job. Nonetheless, the Democrats were shocked, appalled, and put on a show in the hearings and in the press. To this day, despite no evidence other than her own words, the press still reports the events as if they really happened.

Thomas was personally attacked and savaged. Leaders in the black community did not object to the treatment of Thomas. His political leaning trumped his blackness, so treating him in a poor manner was allowed. Thomas got through the conformations, but only after going on the attack by throwing the weapon of race back in the face of Democrats. His famous words, "High-tech lynching," backed Democrats into a corner.

Fast forward a few years, and we have President Bill Clinton. Both in the campaign for President and after winning, Clinton had women accusing him of sexual misconduct. Notice I did not say *woman*, in the singular—such as the case with Justice Thomas. I said *women*. Here is the list:

1. Paula Jones sued Bill Clinton in 1994 for sexual harassment. Jones claims that in 1991 then-Arkansas Governor Bill Clinton propositioned and exposed himself to her in a Little Rock hotel.

2. Juanita Broaddrick, a former nursing home administrator, alleges that Bill Clinton, who was running for Arkansas governor at the time, raped her in an Arkansas hotel room in the spring of 1978.

3. Kathleen Willey was a White House volunteer aide who, in March of 1998, alleged on the TV news program *60 Minutes* that Bill Clinton had sexually assaulted her during his first term as President.

4. Eileen Wellstone, an English woman, alleges that Clinton sexually assaulted her after she met him at a pub near Oxford University where Clinton was a student in 1969.

5. Carolyn Moffet was a legal secretary in Little Rock in 1979, said she met Governor Clinton at a political fundraiser and was invited to his hotel room. Moffet alleges that she fled the hotel room after Clinton demanded she performs sex acts on him.

6. Elizabeth Ward Gracen: A Miss Arkansas who would go on to win the Miss America contest in 1982, Gracen alleges that

she was forced by Clinton to have sex with him shortly after she won the Miss Arkansas competition.

7. Becky Brown: Becky Brown was Chelsea Clinton's nanny. L.D. Brown, an Arkansas State Trooper, and Becky's husband, claims that Clinton attempted to seduce her while the two were in the governor's mansion.

8. Helen Dowdy, the wife of one of Hillary's cousins, alleges that in 1986, Bill Clinton groped her on the dance floor of a wedding.

9. Cristy Zercher was a flight attendant aboard Clinton's campaign jet from 1991-1992. Zercher told the Star magazine that Clinton groped her for over 40 minutes.

Of course, the coup de grace was Monica Lewinsky, whom Clinton told America—with a wagging finger—that he "did not have sex with that woman." That would turn out to be a bald-faced lie, under oath, and led to his impeachment.

Some of the women making the accusations are more credible than others, but what I always found curious was the reaction to all of this from Democrats. The consensus, especially after Lewinsky, was that this is only about sex. It is not important.

Huh?

Let's review; a black man was savaged at the hands of a single accuser with shabby credibility. BUT a possible rape, and certainly using the power of his position on a 22-year-old in Lewinsky, rates nothing? It is just sex. Something that is not important to his job. It's something, in the case of Lewinsky, that all men do. Is it a private manner?

That's what we got from Democrats. Worse, that's what we got from black Democrats. Suddenly, the idea of protecting that oppressed group, women, did not rate as high a priority any more. The same Democrats in politics, television, print media and everyday life, attacked Thomas, hell that attacks him to this day, but poo-poo anything related to Bill Clinton.

In college, I had to take a women's studies class for my major. In the class, the power dynamics between men and women was always a topic of discussion. One of the main tenets postulated by the professor was that when a man is in a position of power and sleeps with an employee, we cannot know if it was consensual. The premise being this: how do we know the woman in question would have slept with the man if he had not been her boss. It was a good question. My professor just did not like me asking her if she applied that same thought process to President Clinton getting "consensual" oral sex in the Oval Office from a 22-year-old intern.

If sexual harassment is wrong, then it is wrong no matter who does it. If you are going to attack a black man based on the word of one woman, then you must attack the white guy who has several women making the same accusation. Why the double-sided treatment?

Make no mistake, if everything was in reverse, if it was a black Democrat being attacked in that manner, the terms racism and racist would be thrown around like a Tom Brady touchdown pass.

As proof, I give you President Barack Obama. No, he has not been accused of any sexual misconduct. However, every criticism of him has been met with accusations of being racially motivated. Do not like Obamacare; then you are racist. Tell the American people he is not qualified, it is because he is black. Think he is stupid for the things he says or does, then it's because you think black people are stupid. YOU ARE A RACIST. Post on Facebook that you think Michelle Obama is a little "thick" to be preaching about eating healthy, you are a racist and a sexist.

That is what you get from white and black Democrats alike. No way are they going to let you attack a black man or woman who is intelligent and accomplished—the caveat being that you get that protection apparently only if you are a Democrat. If you are an accomplished black person who is conservative, then it's hands-off.

Dr. Jeremiah Wright, the infamous former pastor of President Obama, got a lot of attention in the 2008 election because of the words, "God Damn America," and statements about race. What did not get as much attention is what he said about Condoleezza Rice. Dr. Wright referred to Dr. Rice, not as Condoleezza, but as "Condi-skeezer[9]." If you are unfamiliar with black urban street vernacular, a skeezer is a loose woman. A skeezer is worse than a prostitute, because at least the hooker is asking for money. A skeezer will sleep with anyone—and often.

Condi Rice graduated *cum laude* with a B.A. in political science. She has a Masters in the same field, and a Doctorate in International Studies. She has been a diplomat, head of the NSA, and the first black female Secretary of State. She is a concert-level pianist, and has even performed with Yo-Yo Ma. She has been the Provost for Stanford University for years. She is as far as away from the derogatory description of her by Dr. Wright as can be, but he could get away with it. The NAACP did not object. Black congressional members did not say a word. White liberal commentators, who are usually oozing with white guilt, did not appear to notice.

The perennial liberal women's rights group, NOW, had a cow over Rush Limbaugh calling Sandra Fluke a slut, but never uttered a word about the words thrown at Dr. Rice. The definitive black woman's magazine, Essence, not only said nothing, but Dr. Rice has never even graced the cover of their magazine.

---

9   http://ac360.blogs.cnn.com/2008/03/21/the-full-story-behind-wright%E2%80%99s-%E2%80%9Cgod-damn-america%E2%80%9D-sermon/

Yet, somehow, I'm supposed to take seriously from Democrats how they are fighting for *me*? I'm supposed to keep a straight face when a Democrat tells me that Republicans have no respect for blacks?

Let me put this in a different light. Imagine a parent with two kids who are twins. One twin does all the things the parents did in school, and even decides to go to the same college as them. The parents dote on that twin. The other twin does just as well in school as their sibling, but decides to do something different with their life and go to a different school than their parents. Now imagine the parents treating that twin like trash. Instinctively, we know that is wrong. We would all take a dim view of the parents and their attitudes. The same principle is at play here.

You want to know why I'm conservative? Because I know that Democrats do not protect me based on my race. As a child, my mother told me always to treat people well and to gravitate toward the people who treat me well. I was told to surround myself with people who know my character. I know that Democrats do not give a damn about my character. I know that my accomplishments in life do not matter to them. Even if I were to be as perfect as Jesus Christ, but conservative, it is perfectly okay to Democrats to attack me personally, diminish me, and at times, even say racially questionable things to me.

Why the heck would I want to join up for that?

CHAPTER FIVE
No Massa Democrat,
I am NOT a Victim

The number of things that all people—rich or poor, old or young, black or white, American or not American—have in common is astounding. For all the differences, we can find that the list of things we agree on is long. One thing that all people agree on is that when you are facing a tough time in life; you may appreciate empathy and sympathy, but you do not want anyone's pity. There is only one thing more insulting than someone's pity, and that's when they reach out a helping hand filled with patronization.

One of the major political mistakes African-Americans make is being emotional about how they view the two parties. As a people, blacks are emotive. Anything we feel, we do so with passion. Play on our emotions and you have us. The Democrats have been playing the "But we care" card for decades. Overwhelmingly, blacks give Democrats a pass on results, because they believe that they care about the black community and its issues.

Democrats reach out a helping hand with apparent kindness and sympathy. Unfortunately, it is underlain with a feeling of superiority. They are ready to tell you that you need help. And the help you need from them is the help they decide to give you. For example, they will tell you that you need childcare paid for by the government, but not talk about getting a job so that you can pay for your own childcare.

Democrats play identity politics. If you are black, female, gay, Hispanic, illegal immigrant, or the group of choice now, transgender, then you need help fighting for your rights. You are not just being treated unfairly, but you are being oppressed. You are a victim of capitalism and white men. You do not just need help; you need to be saved. And the only way to save you is through the help of Democrats in general, and government specifically.

A Democrat politician steps to the podium and campaigns for more funding for the school, free lunches, and free after-school meals for the poor. They talk about making sure that we have social justice and economic justice. They will extol the need for free health care or social programs, to give the poor and working class a step up the ladder. When a Democrat campaigns, they will tell you that any cut in federal programs is an attack on poor people or minorities; which is code for black people.

That and dozen other things they will tell you the government will do or needs to do. Here is what you do not hear. You never hear them talk about the opportunities that are already around you. You never hear word one about what a person can do *without* the government. You never, ever, hear a speech about what the poor, disadvantaged, or minorities should be doing for themselves. In short, Democrats have twisted President Kennedy's famous words all around. It's no longer "ask what you can for your country." Now the mantra is "demand what your country should be giving you."

I'm conservative; that does not mean I'm blind or ignoring the past. All corporations, government departments and agencies, schools, and universities are made up of people. People have not always done the right, fair, or moral thing in life. If people acted in the correct manner, then slavery would never have occurred. The Jim Crow era is not something we would have a reference point for in American history. Women would have been treated as equals a long time ago. Massive pollution and corporate cover-ups would not have happened.

We have laws for a reason; people break them. There are times when people need to be *forced* to do things, like allowing someone who can afford a house to buy the house. There are groups in this country that have needed the help of the government—no, not the *help*—the *power* of the government to enforce their rights.

I'm a member of one such group. Apart from Native Americans, no other group has been as mistreated for as long as blacks were in the land of the free. It took a Civil War to end slavery. It took a Constitutional Amendment to codify into constitutional law that slavery was illegal. It took hundreds of years and several Civil Rights Acts to codify the rights of blacks, as stipulated in the words and spirit of the Constitution. Americans needed the emotional weight of seeing peaceful marchers, many of whom fought for this country, attacked by fire hoses and dogs—and broadcast on nationwide television—to shame them into realizing racism was wrong.

In each of these instances, the power of government was necessary to make things right. My grandfather was born in 1920. As a young boy and man, he was a victim. His father told him that there were places not to go because he could be killed. There were jobs he would not be able to get because he was black. When he got a job, he was not paid the same amount as a white man. He fought in the war for this country and came back to a country that would not allow him to take a piss in the same bathroom as a white man. My grandfather's life was not unique. His whole generation, as well as the one before him, as well as his own children, experienced racism the way people in a desert experience heat. It surrounds them, determines what they do or cannot do, and permeates their body.

My grandfather needed good people, most of whom were Republicans, to advocate for him. He did not have an even playing field. He did not have equal opportunity.

I am not my grandfather. Neither is any black person born after 1968. None of us has experienced slavery. Not a single black person born after that date has had to live through Jim Crow. The evils of the past have been conquered. The good fight, racial equality, and equal opportunity, was fought and won.

Vann Jones, Touré, anchor Don Lemon, the activists of Blacks Lives Matter, millions of black Generations Xs and black millennials, all have something in common with me. We can all go to the college we want if we have the credentials for entrance. We can live where we want. We can buy whatever car we want. We can walk down the street every day and not hear the word nigger from the people we walk past.

Am I saying that racism does not exist? Of course not. There are still people who have a racial bias for sure. There are people who are racists. They exist, but they do not affect our lives everyday like it did my grandfather. The generation before me fought for me to have what I have. Unlimited possibility, not limited by my race.

The fight was fought and won. Now, all I need from Democrats—all I need from government—is…nothing.

I am not a victim. I reject those who tell me that I am one. No, Democrats or Republicans are not holding me down because I'm black. They can't hold me down.

This is what so many Democrats, especially black ones, do not understand. There are too many systems in place, too many laws, too many good lawyers, too many business owners looking for someone who can help make them even more money, for anyone to hold me back. Sure, a racist cop could stop me and ruin my day. But guess what? A cop who's an asshole can stop a white person and ruin their day. I've been driving a car for three decades plus, and I can count the number of times I've been stopped on just my two hands. That's almost 7,000 days of driving and less than ten stops. I've been black the whole time.

I have an African name, and for many years I sported shoulder-length dreadlocks. I can honestly say I do not think I have ever not gotten a job because I was black. Now, it would be fair to say, "*you would never know. They may have hated your too-ethnic hairstyle, and used an excuse for not hiring you*," and that would be correct. I would not know.

I can say that racism didn't stop me from getting a college degree, or a car, or good job. I have been offered promotions and raises. I have convinced rich white people that the young black guy with a funny name was worthy of their business.

In other words, the degree to which racism in this country still exists does not exist at a level to permanently, or even seriously, impede my life. I am not unique. I am not special. I am not lucky. My overall experience today is the same for all black people.

A black person living in the hood still has more than most immigrants, legal and illegal, have when they get to America. Yet, the success stories of immigrants like Koreans, West Indians, Pakistanis, and Nigerians abound in this country. Many came here with little to nothing, but got educated or started businesses. Now they have homes, cars, money, and good lives. They did not rely on welfare or governmental assistance. Most did not qualify for it. They did not need it. They just needed the opportunity.

Opportunity is the birthright of every American, but especially black Americans. We—meaning our ancestors—bled for it. Now we have it, but one of the political parties wants us to act like we do not. They wish to tell me how, in 2017, my life is adversely affected by slavery; which ended 154 years ago.

My mom wasn't a slave. My grandfather wasn't a slave either. I've never seen a slave. So, how am I the victim of slavery? I have many black friends who have homes. How is racism stopping them? I can point to numerous blacks born in the hood, many of them in my family, who ended up with better lives the moment they decided to not be on government assistance.

The hard reality is that I do not need the Democrats' help. I resent being told by any Democrat, even the black one who used to be President, that without higher taxes, or government subsidized health care, or universal pre-k, that I cannot be successful. I do not need to hear that in order for me to have a fair share and fair shot at the American dream, I need to have just one more program. No. I do not need that. I do not want that.

I will tell you something else, too, and this is the difference. I don't need the Republicans, either. I do not need them to get what I want to have, and Republicans would agree. Republicans have their own programs and ideas, but they center around allowing freedom for people to make their own choices. Yes, that means some people will decide not to buy health care, or go to college, or start a business. They will choose to buy a house they cannot afford, or buy a car they should not have. They will decide not to use birth control. Many people will make bad choices, and Republicans are not going to try and stop them from either the bad choice or the consequences of that choice. And that is the way I like it.

Everything I have and do not have today is because of me. It's not because there is no opportunity. It is not because the white man is holding me down. It is not because of some relative of mine 300 years ago was a slave on a cotton farm. It is not because we just have not let Democrats do all the things they want to do.

I have what I have because of the choices I have made in life.

I do not have many of the things I want, again, because of the choices I have made.

Knowing those two singular facts is empowering. It is up to me. It is in my hands. It does not require a Democrat majority in the House. It does not require a Democrat President. It does not take a new government program to get me over the "hump." Thinking that your fate is dependent on someone else is the very definition of disempowerment. It turns you into a victim.

I do not want to be a victim. I am not a victim. Therefore, I am not a Democrat.

CHAPTER SIX
Success in America is Something You Choose

This chapter deals with perhaps my biggest beef with Democrats. It also happens to be the primary difference between the Democrat/liberal worldview and Republican/conservative worldview. In modern social issues and politics, almost everything can be distilled down to two paths.

Success is either something that is being denied to you, or success is something you choose to pursue. Those are the two competing philosophies.

In college, my professors told me there were still unending barriers to my success because I was black. In the speeches of any Democrat politician, or in conversations I have with everyday black people, success is something that is being kept from me and them. The reason I do not have this or that is because I'm black. An alternative theme is that you do not have the American dream because you are a woman, gay, Spanish, etc.

The American dream is being withheld from you. Or worse, the rich and wealthy are doing all they can to put roadblocks in front of you. The 1% does not care about you. Their lives are blessed and fortunate, but they do not pay their fair share to allow everyone else to have what they were lucky enough to be given in life.

A Democrat would say that characterization is unfair. I would ask them to explain to me the meaning of the words from President Obama, "Fair share and a fair shot," or the words "You didn't build that." I say to any Democrat, tell me why President Obama characterized those with wealth as being selfish, just because they do not wish to pay higher taxes?

I would query the caring and well-intentioned Democrat, why does every conversation about crime in the inner city become a conversation about the lack of opportunity and resources in those communities? How many times must I hear about "white supremacy" or institutional racism as the cause of poor economic statistics within the black community? Why do Nigerians come to America, looking just as black, but have vastly different economic stats?

See, there is a narrative within the progressive mindset that tells me, you, and everyone else who is not a white male, that we just need to fight the appropriate "-ism" for success to be ours. If I'm a child in the hood, then the path out of that life is just another program. We just need another Democrat in office. Let's pass one more new law to fight the oppressor holding me down. Jails are not where they house lawbreakers or those who would do us harm. No, they are the new plantations, where they ship away thousands of young black men.

I'm black. You may be a woman, Spanish, an immigrant, perhaps gay. Sometimes even a white male will make a list if he is dirt poor. We all have something in common, though, and that is Democrats will tell us that it's not our fault. There is something about *us* that prevents success from coming our way. It is who we are that makes others want to make us fail. Worse, the bad things in life—incarceration, poor health, low wages, student loans, even deportation—are things being done to us.

That is the message I hear from Democrats. That is what I take away.

Well, let me tell you something. My name is Kiara Ashanti. I'm a black man in America. I've never been in prison. I've never been arrested for drugs. I have a college degree. I've made minimum wage, and I've made six figures. I have had some really great times in my life. I have also had some totally lousy times in my life. I've had the electric cut off in my apartment, and I've had five figures sitting in my bank account.

In all instances, the good and bad, were not done *to* me. They are things I chose in one way or another. See, what Democrats do not get, but Republicans do, is that life is about choices. Personal responsibility is not a campaign slogan. It is a decision you make to take ownership of your life. It is a choice.

I could be wrong, but I suspect that I'm not in prison for drugs because I do not take drugs. I do not deal drugs. I refuse to associate with anyone who deals drugs, or regularly takes them. I'm not a member of a gang, and so I'm not engaged in illegal activity. Therefore, I have never been in prison. That is a choice I made. I have family members who, in their pasts, made different choices, and paid the price for it. Not because they were black, but because they decided to deal drugs.

I know, I know. Black men get harsher jail sentences than whites do for the same offense. You know what, that is true. Totally wrong. Not fair. Everyone knows that… including the black person who decided to deal anyway. Kids are driving around with a dime bag, and know it is against the law. They have a dime bag anyway. See, you cannot compare modern jails to slavery and plantations because slaves had no choice. Their choice was stolen and then held from them. The young black man in jail had a choice. He could have gone to school, instead of gangbanging. He could have had comic books in a bag instead of weed. He could have decided not to break the law.

When I graduated from high school, I had two choices. I could join the military like my father. Or I could go to college. But guess what? There really was a third choice. I could have chosen to skip both and get a job. Millions of Americans are working in fast food, retail stores, as waiters or dishwashers, or as laborers. They are putting in an honest day's work. It is an honest day's work, however, that does not take any special skill. You don't need a degree or special knowledge to wash dishes, be the fry guy, or mop floors. And so those jobs do not pay much money. Democrats and unions would have you believe that these people are being screwed. We are told that no one can work for nine or ten dollars an hour and raise a family.

I always ask, who put the gun to your head and makes you go to that job? I always query, who put a gun to your head and told you to not go to college? Who told you to drop out of high school? Why have you *decided* to work as the fry guy at McDonald's for ten years?

These were decisions that the person made. It was their choice. "*Well, Kiara, they got pregnant and needed to take care of their child. They needed a job.*" Ok, who told them to have sex without a condom? Who told the male not to bring a condom? Who allowed the male to have sex with them without protection? These are choices. Decisions a person made of their own volition.

This is not a judgment about their character. I am not trying to belittle anyone who is in that circumstance. I am giving them tough love, however. All decisions, good or bad, have consequences. As humans, we love the good consequences and like to use excuses for the adverse consequences. Democrat political thought plays into that weak-minded thought process.

Good choices do not always lead to good outcomes, but bad choices always lead to poor outcomes. When you make a bad choice, the consequences of it are on you.

Southside Chicago is gang-infested and filled with the drugs that gangs sell. Upwards of 40% of black high school kids drop out without graduating. A large population of its residents is on government assistance, as were their parents and grandparents.

There was one girl who did not experience any of that. She decided to stay in school and study hard. She did not take drugs. She did not join a gang. She graduated from high school and went off to college. She did not go to state. No, this young woman got a scholarship to Princeton. She followed that up with a law degree from Harvard. She followed that with a marriage to one man and kids born *within* wedlock. The only thing she did better was becoming the First Lady of the United States.

I'm talking about Michelle Obama. Yeah, she is a Democrat, but it does not change the story. Whatever her Democratic musings that led her to believe she and blacks are victims of *constant* racism, this is not the reason she did not get pregnant in high school, and it is not the reason that friends of hers did. Racism did not lead her onto the path of taking drugs. Yes, she is whip-smart, but do not be fooled. There are millions of whip-smart women in the country who ended up mothers at seventeen, dropped out of school, or are in rehab right now.

Michelle Obama's life is not one of luck—other than marrying the right guy. It is the sum total of the choices she has made. She chose to stay in school. She chose to go to law school.

I'm a smart guy. I thought about going to law school at one point. In fact, it was my plan, but I did not get into the school I wanted. I could have—no, I *should* have—tried again. I should have worked full time, came home at night, studied for the LSAT exam, gotten a better score, and tried to get into law school. I did not do that. I worked and played on the weekends. I spent countless nights pissed off at pretty girls who did not like nice guys like me. I traveled and just lived life without focusing on where I wanted to be in five years.

So, I don't have a law degree. That means for many years in my working life; I did not make as much money as my friends who did go to law school, graduate school, or medical school. Their lives look vastly different from mine.

That is not the fault of white people. That is not the fault of a capitalist system. There was no barrier to me going to law school, or that kept me from it. Some evil white guy is not hidden away in a remote island fortress, laughing manically, as they decide how they are going to screw with Kiara Ashanti's life. That is not how America works today.

Let me tell you about the real America.

America is a ladder. At the bottom of that ladder is a homeless unemployed person with zero income. The top of the ladder is dominated by Bill Gates, with a net worth of 81 billion dollars. In between the two extremes is any income level you want. If you do not like your income level, all you must do is climb up. It is that simple. Really it is.

Simple, however, is not easy. The work comes from making yourself more valuable in the marketplace. A Harvard-educated lawyer is more valuable to an employer than a high-school dropout who mops the floor. Conversely, a metal head, a roughneck, is more valuable on an oilrig than a prissy lawyer from state law school. Why? Because the roughneck has more knowledge of the workings of an oil platform than someone in a suit.

The more value you bring to the marketplace or employer, the more you can earn. It does not take an act of Congress to make $15 dollars an hour. You can go onto Careerbuilder.com right now, and find thousands of jobs that pay $15 an hour. Hell, why settle for that? You can find jobs that pay you $50 dollars an hour. You can find jobs on CareerBuilder that will pay you $200 dollars an hour. It is not a question of whether these jobs exist, they do. The only question is whether or not you have the knowledge, skills, or background to qualify for a job that pays that much per hour.

Right now, there is a niche financial market that, if I entered, would allow me to charge anywhere from $125 to $250 an hour for twenty hours of work—per project. All I need to do is get a certification and hang out my shingle. IF I study for the test. IF I dedicate the hours. IF I CHOOSE to spend my time in that manner, then I can join that profession. All I must do is choose to do what is required, instead of watching television, reading Twitter, or arguing with clueless people on Facebook. Or I can choose to do all those things and not study. If I make the latter choice, then I do not get to make what people in the industry make.

There is a young woman named Kimbra Luna. I heard her being interviewed on a podcast, called Mixergy, about how she went from being on welfare to building a million-dollar business through Facebook. With a lead-in like that, I knew I had to listen to the interview.

Luna is a trainer. She teaches business owners and professionals how to use social media and the internet to market their services. As I listened to her interview and how she built her own business, I did not get a rousing sense of motivation. In fact, I got pissed. Let me give you the broad strokes.

Luna did not graduate from high school. She dropped out and never went back. She obviously never went to college. It should be no surprise that with few job skills, at one point she was on welfare. Now, I do not know Luna's IQ. Maybe she was smart but hated school. There are a lot of people like that. People who are bright, smart, but for whom school is not their thing. Or maybe she wasn't bright from a traditional IQ way of thinking. I do not know. Let me tell you what I do know because of her interview. I have a college degree, and Luna has a million dollars… Actually, Luna has more than one million dollars.

I know Luna started teaching people marketing on the web through the use of webinars, chats, and videos she made with computer screen recorders. She also taught people how to do the same thing for their own businesses. She started doing this in 2010. Everything she was teaching people how to do, and the manner in which was teaching it, I knew how to do back in 2006.

In 2006, I made an interactive e-book with embedded videos and audio in it. I routinely spoke to friends or business associates about how to do webinars on the web, or the best and cheapest way to build a website. WordPress is ubiquitous today, but I knew how to build a kick-ass website on the cheap ten years ago.

There was not a single piece of information she was selling, giving, or showing that I did not already know about. But she had a program that she sold to 460 people at $2,500 a pop, and I did not.

Is there any reason that I could not have done the same thing? It is the same information. I may even have more knowledge in some of those areas than she does. The answer is, of course, no.

In case it is lost on those more inclined to snowflake delicateness, I am not putting Luna down. I'm not saying I am a better person than her because I went to college. I am certainly not saying I'm smarter than Luna.

Luna and I both had knowledge that others did not. We each had skills that others would be willing to pay money to learn. We each had an opportunity to do something with that knowledge beyond casual conversations with random people. Luna took her knowledge and decided to do something with it. I did not.

So, Luna gets to make a couple million a year and hire a nanny to watch her kids while she works. I, on the other hand, get to listen to her interview and get pissed off at myself because I know I could have done the same thing years before her, and did not do it.

BUT, as the line in the movie "The Social Network," goes, "if you could have built Facebook, you would have built Facebook." If I could have built a coaching program and product that made two million a year, then I would have built it.

Life, and certainly not America, does not reward you for what you could have done. It rewards you for what you do. Life rewards action. But more specifically, life rewards the decision to act.

Luna chose to do something with her knowledge. Michelle Obama chose to stay in school. Does that mean they were each guaranteed to end up where they each arrived at in life? No. There are no guarantees in life, except death and taxes; especially when Democrats are in charge. While success is never guaranteed, what is a general rule is that they were going to end up in a better place than where they each started, because they made quality choices.

Many Democrats do not understand that everything we have or do not have in life is determined by what we choose to do or not do. The days where your entire life is controlled and determined by your formal education status, race, sex, etc. are long gone. We have eradicated those issues as *major* barriers.

And I say major because there are individuals in the world who are racist, or sexist. There are people who think that women should not be in certain industries. There are people who believe that black men are all prone to violence, or can't take care of their kids.

I do not have some Kumbaya, Pollyanna worldview where everything is right as rain. Republicans do not believe that either. Those situations happen and must be confronted. But Republicans believe that the ultimate determiner of your state in life and in this country, is you. They want to have systems in place that are fair to everyone regardless of race, religion, sex, or economic status.

Do you think Democrats want everyone to be treated the same? Then why should someone with $100 million dollars pay a higher percentage of their income in taxes than someone at $50,000?

"Well, they have more money."

Why does that have anything to do with it? If everyone paid 25% in taxes, then someone at 50k a yr. would pay $12,500 in taxes, and the $100-million earners would pay $25 million in taxes. Twenty-five million is still higher than $12500.

Perhaps you do not like that example. Okay, try this on for size. Why does an affluent black student have more access to financial aid programs for college than a poor white student? The black family is black but has money. The white student has none.

I can hear my social justice warriors screaming right now. "*They have white privilege!*" Yadda, yadda, yadda. I can assure you that no white person in a trailer park is walking around saying to themselves, "*I may live in a double-wide, but at least I'm white.*"

A level playing field is just that—level. And you cannot ever get to that ideal if a group of people is constantly trying to make the playing field uneven. In the old days, government tilted the odds in favor of white people just because they were white. Today, Democrats want the government to tilt the playing field in the favor of minorities, just because they are black. It is the same damned racist thinking, but in reverse.

Democrats will tell me how much I cannot have in life because I am black, and then try to fix it with racially-based methods. Republicans tell me you can do anything you want, even if you are black. Republicans then try and push programs that allow me the freedom to fly to whatever height my talent, hard work, and decisions can take me.

As I said in the last chapter, one view is disempowering. The other view is empowering.

Tell me, do you want to feel empowered, or without power?

If you want the former, then you must realize that taking personal responsibility and making intentional choices toward success will get you there. If, however, I choose to believe my choices have little bearing on my future, then I'm leaving my future up to someone else. I'm believing the lie that it will take someone else to get me what I want and need in life.

Trust me when I say that having faith in yourself and your own actions will get you where want faster than the opposite. That is my strong belief. That is my world view.

If anything is to be, then it is up to me. I am in control. My success or failure is in my own hands. When you come to believe that, when you inculcate that knowledge into your heart, you cannot be a Democrat.

Because the vast majority of Democrats do not believe your success is up to you.

CHAPTER SEVEN
Shall Not Be Infringed

July 22, 2007

Dr. William Petit has just enjoyed a lazy Sunday afternoon with his wife Jennifer and two young daughters, Hayley and Michaela. His wife has cooked a great family meal. His daughter Michaela has snuggled into bed with Jennifer. It's an endearing move that her mother knows will not last long. Michaela is 11 and on the cusp of adolescence. Soon the habits of a child will vanish before the onslaught of teenaged independence and angst.

Unfortunately, the sweetness of a child lying next to a parent and the tranquility of a lazy Sunday would end abruptly. At 3am, two men invaded the Petit home. They woke Dr. Petit with a baseball bat to the head and demanded money; they also ordered Dr. Petit to open his safe. What followed in the early morning hours into the middle of the day is the stuff of nightmares. Dr. Petit was beaten and tied to a chair. His wife Jen was taken to a bank in the morning for money. Jen managed to alert a teller of the situation, but it did not prevent her from being taken home, raped, and then killed. That same fate happened to her two daughters; Dr. Petit was tied in the basement of his home, but heard the brutal rapes above him. When the intruders were done, they doused the floors around the two girls' beds with gasoline and set the house on fire. Dr. Petit was the only survivor.

December 31st, 2011

Sarah McKinley is 18, but not out celebrating the end of the year. McKinley is recovering. Her husband passed only a week ago, after losing a fight with cancer. She is grieving, but her focus is more on her three-month-old baby. She is now a single mother.

A week earlier, a man named Justin stopped by the house, claiming to be a friend of her husband. Sarah did not recognize him, and therefore did not let him in the house. Her husband had been on strong painkillers, and Sarah suspected the man was looking for the leftover drugs. On New Year's Eve, Justin returned in the dead of night with a 12-inch hunting knife and another man. They broke into Sarah's home.

Sarah called 911, but being in a rural area, she and the 911 operator knew the sheriff would not reach her home in time. It did not matter. Sarah had a baby and her life to protect. She also had a 12-gauge shotgun.

November 2, 2016

On November 2, Sherri Papini was jogging like millions of other women do every day. Her morning routine was interrupted when she was attacked and abducted. She was found alive twenty-two days later, 120 miles from where she was attacked. Authorities have no suspects, though Papini claims she was taken by two Hispanic women. Police are also puzzled at why she was released. The one thing they do know is that Papini is lucky. Nine other women from her area had been kidnapped, and all nine had been killed. Sherri and all nine of the other victims lives in California. They also have one other thing in common—none of them were armed.

These are three stories. They are just three among the thousands that I could recount here for you if I choose. Stories of Americans attacked in their homes, or on the street and killed. Stories of Americans attacked in their homes, or on the street, but many are alive today because they had a gun.

According to the Centers for Disease Control (CDC), the number of people who have needed to use a gun as a defensive measure can range from 500,000 to as high as 3 million a year[10]. That is not a small range, but even if you take the lowest estimate, it means over the decades, millions of lives have been saved from death or harm because of a gun.

That should surprise you because the media does not report these events often enough. Occasionally a story will pop up on local news, but the major networks reserve their gun stories for events like Sandy Hook, Chicago weekend death totals, or other mass shootings. The overwhelming viewpoint within the news media is that guns are a problem. The only thing worse are the people who fight to keep guns easy to obtain, restrict "common sense" gun restrictions, and who support gun rights.

As a party, Democrats can be seen as the party of three major issues: increasing taxes constantly on the rich, abortion, and restricting guns. Most Democrats do not like guns, and believe that America should do what the countries England, Japan, or Australia have done, and outlaw them. Some Democrats will say, "No, we do not want to take your guns, but you don't need military-style assault weapons." The AR-15 is the most hated gun among liberals currently, and its use in the tragedies like Sandy Hook and San Bernardino offer examples of why they feel that way. Further, there are the almost 34,000 deaths by guns a year in the U.S. Another 73,000 non-fatal injuries occur from firearms each year[11].

---

10 http://www.cnsnews.com/news/article/cdc-study-use-firearms-self-defense-important-crime-deterrent
11 https://www.cdc.gov/nchs/fastats/injury.htm

Couldn't we avoid those deaths and injuries if fewer people had guns? Shouldn't we do all we can to keep children from getting gunned down by an AR-15 assault rifle? Shouldn't we all agree, Republican and Democrat alike, that universal background checks is something that we should have before the purchase of a gun?

These are all good questions, and the answer to them really depends on what you believe. Democrats love to quote stats and the heartbreaking stories of people killed by a firearm. Politicians like Michael Bloomberg, Diane Feinstein, and activists like Shannon Watts demonize the NRA and gun owners as "evil people," or "in the pockets of gun manufacturers," but have never spoken to a woman who is alive today because of her gun. How many Dr. Petits or Sherri Papinis of the world have they spoken to? Why is it so easy for any gun control activists to find the crying mother of a child who has been killed by a gun, but cannot run into a mother who is alive today because they had a gun to protect themselves? Both stories are valid and both viewpoints should be sought out and told.

The issue of guns in America is complicated to many people. It is not complicated to me. I have a philosophy that says you always stay with first principles. When in a debate or moral crisis, you center yourself by going back to the root cause, philosophy, or principle at play in the situation. If you do that, then what to do and believe becomes crystal clear.

In the case of guns, that means ignoring what the Republicans say *and* what the Democrats say. Push the rhetoric aside and ask the simple question, "Why are guns even legal in America?" and "What is the purpose behind their legality?" Those are the only two questions that matter. Everything else is either an argument in support of the answers to those questions, or a temper tantrum against the answers simply because you do not like them.

The United States Constitution is the law of the land and serves as the foundation for this country. Every right we have is derived from that document. The men who wrote the document sat for weeks, debating and discussing what would be the founding principles of the new nation called America.

The first and most important right they declared each American would have was freedom of speech. Each of us, you and I, can say whatever we want about our leaders. It can be rude, mean, nasty, racist, sexist, or plain dumb. It does not matter. We can say it, and those who do not like it must find a way to get over it.

The second right enumerated, meaning the second most important to all the founders, was the right to bear arms. That right is written like this:

A well-regulated Militia, being necessary to the security of a free State, the right of the people to keep and bear Arms, shall not be infringed.

Democrats have often tried to argue that the words are only talking about the right to have an armed militia, which would be unnecessary today because we have police to protect us. Unfortunately, the people who make this argument do not understand basic grammar. The comma means there is a break in the sentence and is used when listing separate items. So, the second amendment is a list of three things separate from each other. A militia, the right to keep and bear Arms, and that neither shall be infringed upon. It is the last part that matters most. The word "infringe" means to "act so as to limit or undermine (something), to encroach on."

With that definition in mind, the last part of the Second Amendment means the aforementioned rights—a militia and the peoples' right to keep and bear arms—shall not be limited, undermined, or encroached on. That is the first principle. Everyone in America has a right to own a firearm. The government has *no authority* to limit that right, or take it away, short of a Constitutional Amendment outlawing guns.

This is the key to understanding anything else. Sure, there are a lot of gun laws in America. There is the assault weapons ban, laws restricting magazine sizes, laws on who can buy a gun and who cannot, and laws that only allow some people to buy certain classes of guns versus others. All of them have been argued in court; most are flawed laws that are flatly unconstitutional.

Yes, we have laws today (and not just about guns) that violate the first set of laws the country had—the Constitution. How have they been justified? The answer is the idea of a living Constitution.

Liberals and Progressives believe and want things that are not advocated for or allowed in the Constitution. Further, there are situations like abortion or gay marriage, for example, which are not addressed in the Constitution. Those situations are supposed to be left up to the states; meaning if the state of California wants to allow or ban something not governed by the Constitution, they can do that. California can have gay marriage, and Alabama can decide not to allow gay marriage. Liberals do not like that, so that idea of a living Constitution was formed.

The Living Constitution doctrine says that the meaning of the Constitution changes with the times. The words do not mean what they say. They mean what they would mean in modern times. If that feels or sounds a little convoluted, that is because the idea is totally stupid. For example, at one point slavery was legal. Per amendments to the Constitution, it is now illegal. If you believe the living constitution theory, that means in the future, slavery could be legal again. I know it feels like, "Oh my God, people would never do such a thing again." But people did it, to begin with so yes, it is possible.

The point, however, is that using the living constitution theory, a lot of gun laws have been put into place. Further, it is the basis for gun rights advocates to enact more gun laws.

The Constitution gives me the clear right to own a gun if I want. Any person, organization, or political party that tries to restrict or take away that right is not worthy of support. Let me be clear; there is no difference between trying to take away the second amendment and restricting the first amendment. If you can ignore the second amendment, then you can ignore the thirteenth amendment that outlaws slavery.

Democrats wish to tell me whether I can have a gun (try to buy a handgun in DC or Maryland), what type of gun I can have, or what I need it for. Activists love saying, "No one needs an AR-15," or in regards to a concealed carry permit, Congressman Charlie Rangel has said, "I wouldn't let them have it… law-abiding citizens just shouldn't have to carry a gun."

The bottom line is that Democrats don't get to make those decisions for me. I don't have to *need* an AR-15 or a handgun to own one. All I need is the desire to own it. Maybe I want to hunt, or competition shoot, or just look at it because I think it's pretty. It does not matter why I want it; the Constitution says if I want it, I can have it. Period, end of story. If I want one, or a hundred, I get to have either. That's called freedom. That's called America.

What do Republicans say? Republicans fight for the words in the Constitution. Every American citizen has a right to a gun, and so the government should not be interfering with that. They say people in crime infested cities: Chicago, Detroit, South Central LA, South Philly, Camden, N.J., should be able to have a gun to protect themselves. Interestingly, all the cities I mentioned are Democrat-run, and have strong gun restrictions, but still have high crime rates. Republicans support the NRA, which is *the oldest* civil rights organization in the country. They don't fight for guns; they fight for the second amendment, which allows you to own a gun. They are protecting your Constitutional rights. The real question for Democrats is: Why aren't they protecting my constitutional rights?

Perhaps it's their racist history. During the civil rights fight, blacks were being beaten and lynched throughout the South by the KKK. Some blacks applied for permits for guns to protect themselves. They were turned away, including Dr. Martin Luther King. The Alabama authorities at the time considered him "unsuitable" to own a gun. The NRA fought these restrictions and helped blacks form NRA chapters, and get a hold of guns. The most famous of these historical situations occurred in Monroe, NC, where Robert F. Williams fought the KKK with the help of the NRA, and armed blacks. His story is recounted in his book, "Negroes with Guns[12]."

I find it curious that in the civil rights era, Democrats fought against my right as a black American to own a gun. And in 2017 Democrats… still fight against my right to own a gun. At least now they are also trying to restrict the rights of white Americans to own a gun as well, so perhaps we have progress. The Democrat party is finally trying to restrict the rights of all Americans equally.

As a young man growing up, I did not think of this issue in these terms. My mother did not own a gun. The only firearm I ever saw was my grandfather's shotgun in a gun rack. But my mother never bad-mouthed the idea. Perhaps it was because she was a military spouse. Or maybe it was not a concern because we lived in the suburbs, and she was not worried about me getting caught up with a gang. It is even fair to say, I've never had a family member or loved one killed in a mass shooting. Fair point.

You know what I do have though? I have friends who have been raped—more than one. I also have a vivid imagination, and so the idea of any of my family members or friends being confronted in a situation like Dr. Petit or Sarah McKinley is unacceptable. If it were up to me, every woman in America would have a gun, and

12 https://www.amazon.com/Negroes-Guns-Robert-F-Williams/
dp/1614274118

would be able to shoot it as well as they walk in high-heeled shoes. I'd rather have a gun and never need it, than to need it and not have it.

The whole idea behind gun rights is that people all have a natural right to self-defense. We all have natural rights, like to not be a slave, and the right to defend yourself from harm. You also have the right to defend yourself from oppression. Considering that the colonies were breaking away from England, whom they considered an oppressive force in their lives, it is little wonder that they made a law that says you cannot infringe on the right of an American to own a gun.

The world is full of bad people. There are rapists, murderers, and criminals out in the country who wish to do others harm. There are now terrorists in our midst who want nothing more than to kill infidels. We are beyond the second amendment being an entitled right to every American. We are now in a world where we each need to own one, because every day that we do not have an attack is a lucky day.

Would guns solve all violent crime? No, of course not. Criminals are not rational thinking people. If they were, they would not be criminals. If everyone had a gun, there are those who would still try to harm you, rob you, and assault you. Home invasions would still occur, but the lauded stats that liberals try and use so often do not lie. States with more constitutionally-based laws on guns have less crime, and fewer deaths by guns. Democrats like to cite the 33,000 gun deaths, but most of those are by suicide. Per the CDC report, "Between the years 2000 and 2010, firearm-related suicides significantly outnumbered homicides for all age groups, annually accounting for sixty-one percent of the more than 335,600 people who died from firearm-related violence in the United States.[13]"

What about the deaths that are caused by guns? Southside Chicago was up to approximately 400 murders by the end of 2016.

13 https://www.cdc.gov/mmwr/preview/mmwrhtml/rr5214a2.htm

Shouldn't we make it harder for criminals to get guns? We should sure as hell try to do that. Now if someone could just explain to me how creating a law that restricts the rights of "law abiding" Americans makes us safer from criminals who ignore the law?

I've never understood this reasoning. Democrats always seem to act as if criminals follow the law. If we took AR-15s away tomorrow, what would that do to criminals? Not a damned thing. The assault weapons ban went into effect in the 90s—did that stop mass shooting? Oh right, we still have the AR-15. Tell me, those 400-plus deaths by guns in Chicago, were they committed with AR-15s?

Here is a stat from the FBI, just to give a little context. The FBI does not track deaths by the sub category of AR-15s, but they do track the number of deaths by rifle; which ARs fall under. In 2014, the number of deaths tracked to a rifle was 251. The number of people killed by physical assault, 670[14].

Here is another one. The Washington Post did a story on the total number of people killed in mass shootings. They defined a mass shooting as any event with four or more people killed. Their starting point was the year 1966. The total that year was 881 people. Not a small number. Nonetheless, in 2016, 3,164 people died, per the Dept. of Transportation, because of texting and driving. That's right. Your little smart phone is responsible for more deaths each year than an AR-15.

Naturally, that means we ought to ban cell companies from allowing the ability to text from cell phones, right?

Now people will say that those two things are not equivalent comparisons. I cannot just take out my phone and start shooting people. However, that is myopic thinking. End results matter more than rare, one-off events. Texting will kill more people than assault weapons. Banning either would not do anything about it.

14 https://www.washingtonpost.com/graphics/national/mass-shoot-ings-in-america/

And this is the last reason that makes me choose Republican over Democrat. You cannot control peoples' behavior. Laws—of any kind—exist as deterrents to people making illegal choices in their lives, but they cannot force people to follow them.

Guns don't kill people, people do. They can use a gun, or knife, or their hands. If they want to kill someone, they are going to do it. If a man wants to rape a woman, he is going to try. A burglar who wants what's in your house is going to try and break in. An ex/boyfriend/husband who wants to beat his lover/girlfriend/wife is going to do it. When that happens, what options do you want the victim to have at their disposal to prevent their death?

Democrats want people to be better. Republicans want you to be able to stop the people who are not trying to be better. See, ultimately this issue is rooted in reality. Criminals don't listen to the law, and I need a way to protect myself. Republicans understand that. Democrats don't seem to. Republicans are fine with what the constitution says, "the right to bear arms, shall not be infringed." Democrats always to use the law to stop what they think is bad. They ignore the Constitution—until it suits their purpose, like in abortion or gay marriage—because they think they can stop bad things from happening to people with just a piece of paper. Or because they overreact when a mass shooting occurs, but never ask about the single mom sitting at home with her kids. Don't they deserve protection as well?

The answer is yes, and the Constitution gives them an unquestioned option for them to help themselves. Republicans follow that. Democrats do not.

And that is why I choose the Republican way.

CHAPTER EIGHT

RESULTS ARE THE NAME OF THE GAME

"Insanity: doing the same thing over and over again and expecting different results."

-Albert Einstein

This famous quote forms the foundation for one of my enduring frustrations when it comes to my fellow blacks and Democrats. The whole premise of this book, "Why am I a conservative," is only necessary because everyone knows that blacks are Democrats and it's odd to find a black person who is not. If a white person says they are a Republican, there is not likely to be an exclamation of surprise from another white person. If there is any reaction at all, it will stem from a disbelief in the policies, not a reaction of surprise.

Why is that the case? America is 241 years old; for 190 of those years, the public rhetoric from Democrats could only be seen as racist. The party was not founded by blacks. The party is not filled to the brim with blacks. Before Barack Obama, there were no black senators. There are only 45 black congressmen as of 2017, and the majority of them are from black districts. So, if it is not because they receive overwhelming electoral positions from whites, and it's not the historical deeds of the Democrat party, what could it be? All you are left with, on the surface, are the policies of one party versus the other.

The purpose of representative government, as conceived originally at America's founding, is for the people to have a say in the laws that govern them. They want a say in whether we go to war, or what is legal versus illegal in their country. As the country matured, society became more sophisticated, and the economic systems became more complex, the government also turned into a mechanism for making people's lives better. If there is a problem, many people look to government for a fix.

There are ongoing arguments about the degree to which the government should be involved in education, healthcare, economics, and social issues, but the government is involved. Therefore, it would make sense for any group to support the political party that is pushing laws or policies that make their lives better. It is that last part that matters and is most puzzling regarding African-Americans. The black community has given the Democrats unwavering support since the mid-sixties, but the policies of the Democrats have not turned the black community into beacons of hope and success.

Below is a chart that tracks the top cities for African-Americans.

10 Cities with Highest Percentage of Blacks or African Americans

City 2000	%	City 2010	%
Gary, Ind	84.0	Detroit, Mich	82.7
Detroit, Mich	81.6	Jackson, Miss	79.4
Birmingham, Ala	73.5	Miami Gardens, Fla	76.3
Jackson, Miss	70.6	Birmingham, Ala	73.4
New Orleans, La.	67.0	Baltimore, Md.	63.7
Baltimore, Md	64.3	Memphis, Tenn	63.3
Atlanta, Ga	61.4	New Orleans, La	60.2
Memphis, Tenn	61.4	Flint, Mich	56.6
Washington, DC	60.0	Montgomery, Ala	56.6
Richmond, Va	57.2	Savannah, Ga.	55.4

*Cities with 100,000 people or more

Source: U.S. Census Bureau, Census 2000; The Black Population: 2010

In addition to these, famous cities such as Los Angeles, Chicago, New York, and Philadelphia also have large inner cities with high black populations; places like Southside Chicago, South Philly, South Central, and Oakland. Most of these cities have the following in common:

- High crime
- High high-school dropout rate
- Lower average wages, as compared to areas surrounding them
- All show up with schools rated as the worst in the country[15]*
- High general and youth unemployment
- High percentage of population receiving some form of public assistance
- The black areas within each have been presented as, and have been Democrat run for the last 50 years

Question, when you are looking to move into a new neighborhood and the real estate agent is trying to sell you on the area, do you want to hear, "Oh, yes, it has a lot of crime, plenty of gangs, average-to-failing schools, and no decent jobs close by?" No, those are not community selling points.

To be fair, these problems are not just in pre-dominantly black communities. There are plenty of white rural areas that have the same problems; some are probably Republican districts. However, white people do not vote for one party as a block—black people do.

There is a host of reasons for the results in the cities listed above, but what about how black people are doing as a general part of the population? Here are a few bullet points[16].

- Median income for blacks $43,300 vs $71,300 for whites
- Poverty rate for blacks 26.2% vs. 10.1% for whites

15 https://www.neighborhoodscout.com/blog/top-100-worst-schools
16 http://money.cnn.com/2015/11/24/news/economy/blacks-whites-inequality/

- Average household family wealth $7,113 for blacks vs. $111,146 for whites
- Homeowners for blacks is 42% vs. 71% for whites
- Unemployment for blacks (2015) 9.2% vs 4.4% for whites

Those are the economic stats. On the social front, only 29% of blacks were married as of 2014. The out-of-wedlock rate for blacks is 70%; that means seventy percent of black children are being raised without a father in the household. In 1964, that number was only 24%. If you want a comparison number, the rate of out-of-wedlock births for whites is 18.1%.

On the educational front, the stats are interesting. Take a look at this chart from the U.S. Census Bureau.

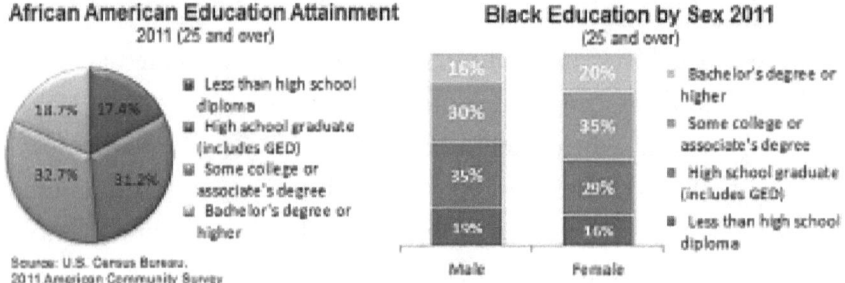

African American Education Attainment
2011 (25 and over)

- Less than high school diploma
- High school graduate (includes GED)
- Some college or associate's degree
- Bachelor's degree or higher

18.7% 17.4%
32.7% 31.2%

Source: U.S. Census Bureau.
2011 American Community Survey

Black Education by Sex 2011
(25 and over)

Male: 16%, 30%, 35%, 19%
Female: 20%, 35%, 29%, 16%

- Bachelor's degree or higher
- Some college or associate's degree
- High school graduate (includes GED)
- Less than high school diploma

The distribution between dropouts, some college, four-year degrees, and graduate degrees is relatively even. It is not what you would expect when considering the high-school dropout rates in predominantly black cities and areas. The dropout rate in places like Chicago, Detroit, and other inner cities is upwards of 30%-plus. For the national stats of blacks without high school diplomas to drop to 19% and 16%, a significant number of blacks who do not live in the inner city are graduating from high school. There could be a number of factors for this: better incomes, better schools, or more importantly, two-parent households. The truth might be that's its all of those things.

What matters here, though, is one single question. *Why are all the stats related here not better?* Democrats have been in charge of those areas for the last half-century. They control the policies, the funding, they work with the unions, and they fight for national policies that fight poverty. They are the war dogs for blacks, but are any of those numbers in economics, wealth, or education numbers to be proud of in America? Perhaps I expect too much, but given the amount of time Democrats spend talking about how their policies are much better for black and brown people, why are these high-population black neighborhoods and cities not as successful as predominantly white or mixed communities?

I expect that some would say that it shows racism is still a part of the American fabric. An argument could be made that the disparity in all areas is so large, only race can be offered as a cause. Such was the case in college from my professors and fellow black college students. Liberal pundits and intelligentsia like Dr. Marc Lamont Hill, Michal Eric Dyson, Van Jones, Cornell West, and others make this argument all the time. As far as they are concerned, social justice has not been delivered to the black community.

There are a couple of problems with this view. One, it is based on emotional reactions to national averages. Averages do not tell the story—at least not accurately.

Statistics that are used correctly compare equal things. You do not compare the health of, say, a cancer patient with the health of a disease-free 20 yr. old. That would seem to be common sense. Why then only look at the average of white incomes versus black incomes? Would it not make more sense to compare the income of white college graduates to the incomes of black college graduates?

Which brings me to problem two. The liberal intelligentsia either has not done what is called a regression analysis in these areas, or they have ignored the results. When you compare a black person with a four-year degree to a white person with a four-year degree, something interesting happens. The difference in income is within 95% of each other. See the chart below.

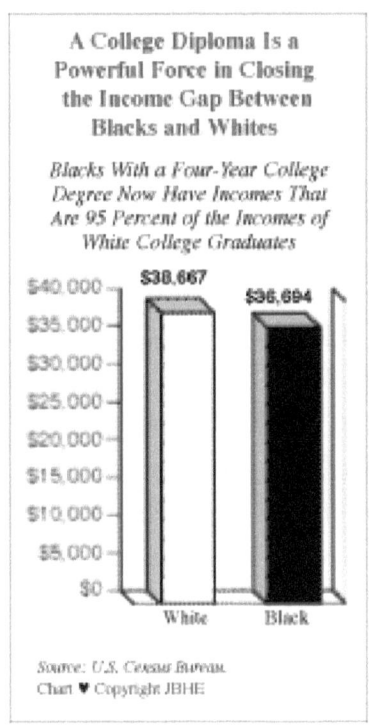

A College Diploma Is a Powerful Force in Closing the Income Gap Between Blacks and Whites

Blacks With a Four-Year College Degree Now Have Incomes That Are 95 Percent of the Incomes of White College Graduates

Source: U.S. Census Bureau.
Chart ♥ Copyright JBHE

The chart of that information is a little dated, 2003, but has the country changed at a fundamental level since then? No, it has not. So, it is reasonable to assume the differences are still small, or closer. I could write a whole book or academic study that digs into the differences between blacks and whites at equivalent education and background levels. Lucky for you that is not the purpose of this book. I'm just reporting what the general surface level issues are, and asking the question, "What is there that is so great in order for me to give the Democrats my heart and soul?"

Remember, my mother raised me to think, "show me." That is one of many gifts she gave me. I will believe anything you want, as long as you can show me. If you cannot, then the question is not "why I do not believe, it is *why do you believe?*"

BUT, for the sake of argument, let's say it was racial animus by a not-insignificant number of white people in the country. Shouldn't all the policies and money that Democrats spend to correct social and racial inequities—real or perceived—have fixed it? In other words, if you need welfare, affirmative action, racially-specific college admissions, and scholarships to make up for racism, then shouldn't they have made up for racism? President Johnson started the so-called War on Poverty in 1964, and we have spent almost 22 trillion to combat it. Three years after the social welfare programs started, the poverty rate was 15%. In 2016, the rate of poverty in the U.S. was…15%[17]. So…trillions of dollars later, we have the same rate of poor people in the America. I don't know about you, but that sounds like a fail to me.

Whenever this simple fact is brought up, there are those who like to point to the fact that today's population is quite higher than in 1964. America has over 320 million people today; in 1964 the population was only 191 million. Proponents of the war on poverty will say that without that money, poverty would be higher. I do not think that argument tracks. One, you cannot know for certain that is the case. It is truly an unknowable fact, but this is a debate tactic Liberals like to use often: "If we did not do 'x,' it would have been worse." You see this argument used with Obamacare and the trillion-dollar stimulus after the Mortgage Meltdown. The 60s had more farmers than now. They had whole segments of the population that could not fully engage in the workforce, like blacks and women. As those avenues opened for those groups, and we became more industrialized, the number of people in poverty

17 http://www.heritage.org/poverty-and-inequality/report/the-war-poverty-after-50-years

would not have been high regardless of the money, in my opinion. Blacks provide a perfect example of this.

In 1966, the poverty rate for blacks was 41.8%. That number has fallen to 27.1% today[18]. An unquestionable success, correct?

Umm, no. Look at the start date again: 1966. What was happening in 1966? America was just moving into a post-Civil Rights world. Opportunities for jobs, housing, and education were just being opened up by force of law. Race still kept blacks from certain jobs and industries. Over the decades, blacks have moved into those areas. The availability of open opportunities has more to do with the drop in poverty than government programs does.

In addition, how does a racist white person cause anyone to decide to have sex without a condom or birth control, and get pregnant? Does the KKK show up in the house of the father, and threaten them into not marrying the mother?

This is what I'm driving at with all that background. Given the level of loyalty blacks have to Democrats, I expect more to point to as a reason for it. We fight for the same policies, keep Democrats in power in our predominantly black cities, but we don't have any appreciable results in those areas. In other words, we are insanely doing the same thing as a community, but expecting different results.

I have basic questions for people who tell me that Democrat policies are better. If that is true, then why were the schools in the inner cities bad 50 years ago, and after 50 years of Democrat governance, still bad today? Why is there no industry, and minimal job prospects, in cities like Detroit and Flint, Michigan? Why am I more likely to get shot and killed in predominantly black Southside, Chicago than a town in Georgia that used to have the KKK?

I could ask a thousand more such questions. The bottom line is that in life, results is the name of the game. The results all blacks desire for their community is not present in places where everything

---

18 http://www.pewresearch.org/fact-tank/2014/01/13/whos-poor-in-america-50-years-into-the-war-on-poverty-a-data-portrait/

is done according to Democrat policy and liberal philosophy. That is an unquestioned fact. When confronted with that fact, liberals usually resort to saying that is because not enough has been done.

What the hell else do you want to do?

I believe there are two fundamental reasons for the political mistakes African-Americans make. The first is an emotional one. There is an old saying that goes, "They don't care what you know until they know you care." It is an old standby line for teaching public speakers about how to connect with their audience. If the audience does not think or feel you care, then they tune you out.

African-Americans think that Democrats care about them.

It seems trite, but it is the God's honest truth. Blacks feel that Democrats want to help people, while Republicans do not. Republicans are considered heartless because they do not want to spend money on programs for people. Republicans are cold because we want people to be self-reliant. Republicans preach "personal responsibility," which many people see as code for judgmental and "your circumstances are your own fault." Most of the economic principles that conservatives believe in are most helpful to those who own businesses. Most of the people in the world who are rich are business owners. Therefore Republicans are for the rich, not the poor and infirm. Those are the beliefs attached to Republicans.

What is crazy and unfortunate is that this emotional response was a total political calculation. It was planned for and anticipated.

Before the Civil Rights movement, most blacks were Republicans. The Democrats, as related in this book ad nauseum, were not in the corner for blacks—not as a party. After Kennedy was killed, now President Johnson needed a political win for the country. Kennedy was slowly working for the Civil Rights Act, behind the scenes, and getting it signed into law was a way to glob onto Kennedy's popularity and the emotion of his assassination.

Johnson, who up until then had been a raving racist, publicly supported the legislation. Even though the Republicans are responsible for getting the bill to his desk, the law of politics dictates that the President gets the blame and credit for what happens on his watch. Johnson signed the Civil Rights Act into law and followed that up with the War on Poverty initiatives. The social welfare programs were not specifically targeted to blacks per se, but given the economic status of a community that had been boxed out of the economic process for decades, many of the reforms applied to the black community.

Johnson knew what he was doing. Get a group, any group, dependent on something you created, and they will always be with you. At this point, I'm going to give a quote that President Johnson is known to have uttered, after the signing of the Civil Rights Act and War on Poverty programs. I will not censor the quote, because you need to understand the evil that lies beneath it.

"I'll have those Niggers voting Democratic for 200 years."

Johnson is said to have uttered these words to two Southern governors on Air Force One. The quote was first reported by a journalist, Ronald Kessler, in his book, *Inside the White House*. Kessler says his secret service contacts relayed the information to him. Democrats, not surprisingly, dispute the quote. Kessler, however, is no conservative and is known as a fine journalist. More important, it is widely known that Johnson was quite liberal with his use of the terms "niggers" and "negroes" in everyday conversation. So, it is not outside of the realm of believability. Plus, what has happened since the mid-1960s? Blacks have voted Democrat at a level of around 90 percent in all elections: local, state and federal.

The second mistake is one of human nature. It is human nature to always veer toward the easy route. Parents know this. Will a child clean their room on their own, or let mom and dad do it if mom and dad always do it? If a teenager can get away with someone else doing their homework for them, will they refuse and do it on their own? No, they will allow someone else to do it, while they surf the web or post on social media.

It is easier to accept massive public programs than it is to say, "What can we do ourselves?" or "What problems are we creating?" The idea of a public safety net is an admirable concept, especially for a country as rich as America. The problem is that public assistance can become a way of life.

I have worked in the "hood." I have been in the projects, and Section 8 housing of inner cities. I have been in the apartment complexes where every resident is on Medicaid and receiving food stamps. I was always struck by how many of my Medicaid clients had better furniture than me. I was always puzzled about the general health of the women and men. Only small portions of any of the people in those neighborhoods are the old, disabled, or infirm. I was not constantly seeing seniors in their 60s, living on small social security benefits. Most of the people were young mothers. Many of them had mothers who had been on public assistance as well. It has become a lifestyle for many in America, because it is easier. When you are constantly given something, and not required to step up, you don't step up.

When I first graduated from college, I had no idea what I wanted to do. I had planned on law school, but I had not gotten in to where I wanted to go, and so was a bit lost. I got part-time jobs. I tried to run my own businesses, but I was not focused. I often had to ask my mother for money to help with my bills.

My mother was getting up in age, and I was her first born. She was not as stringent with me as she was when I was young. Finally, one day my stepfather (who married my mother while I was in college, and so did not raise me) pulled me aside. He told me, in no uncertain terms, that these problems were my problems. I was young, smart, and healthy. I needed to be more responsible and make better decisions. They would help me that month, but no more. That was it.

My mother remained silent, something she never was when I was growing up. I'm sure they had an argument about what he was going to tell me, but she deferred to him. Probably because she knew he was right. To my credit, I did not blow up. I did not go on some rant about him not being my father.

I went out and got a real job. I started being more careful about my money and expenses. I basically started acting like an adult. I did that because the safety net was removed. I could not rely on them to save me. I would need to step up to the plate.

Public policy is the same way. No, we cannot just erase all public assistance. We can make it more difficult just to get it and remain on it. When President Clinton signed the Welfare-to-Work reforms into law in the 90's, liberals predicted massive doom. There would be kids starving in the streets and homelessness would skyrocket.

Neither event occurred. What actually happened is more people ended up in jobs that allowed them to get off of welfare completely. The welfare rolls went down from 12 million to 4 million in 2012[19]. More unmarried women got jobs. The number of children living in poverty dropped.

The results were not all positive. A compromise in the bill allowed states to divert the money paid out in welfare payments to other poverty programs. In no shock to anyone, those programs saw an increase in funding and utilization. That is not a good thing, because welfare programs of any sort are not designed to get you off the program. They are another form of drug habit. Once you are on them, there is nothing inherent in them that moves you into self-sufficiency.

---

19 http://dailysignal.com/2012/07/19/family-fact-of-the-week-how-welfare-reform-helped-families/

Why Democrats always fight to keep people on the programs, rather than wanting them off of them, I do not know. Smarter people than me have tried to puzzle that out, and have come to no definitive conclusion. I just know that when I look at someone who is on public assistance at age twenty, and where they are a decade later, their life is no better, unless they are not on public assistance and taking personal responsibility. When people start making positive choices in their behavior, spending, and life choices, their lives get better. Their lives do not get demonstrably better if they get onto another program from Uncle Sam.

Democrats have created a lot of programs for the poor and minority communities. Yet, fifty years after the beginning of these programs, they campaign for more programs. It seems to me that if the previous programs and policies had worked, then you would not need new ones. Think about it. If you go to the mechanic to fix something in the car, and the same problem happens over and over again, how long does it take you to decide to go to another mechanic?

Democrats preach helping the black community. Hell, they preach about helping all communities. But when I look at the communities that rely on them most, black or white, those communities are not better off. I do not see the results. I do not see anything getting repaired. All I see is my people, African-Americans, running back to the mechanic and saying, "this is still not fixed." I want something better in life for my fellow black people, and so I cannot in good conscious be a Democrat.

As long as blacks ignore the results, and focus on the belief that Democrats care and that is enough, things will not get better. I do not care that Democrats, especially the rank-and-file ones, have good intentions. Results matter, not intentions. "The road to Hell is paved with good intentions," and hell is exactly what many blacks living in Democrat run areas are living through every day.

CHAPTER NINE
I'm Nobody's Uncle

Urban Dictionary: "Sell-Out"—Someone who forgets their roots, or anyone who sacrifices their integrity for success or money.

If you ever have occasion to speak to someone who is an anthropologist, ask them how ancient man managed to survive. Think about it; we are not particularly strong as compared to other mammals, we do not have fur, we have no fangs or claws. We are not fast. Anyway, you cut it, we should be at the lower end of the animal domination pole.

The obvious answer is that we are smarter than animals. We can use tools in ways they cannot. That is true. It is also true, and I'm sure anthropologists would point it out, it was a long time before we mastered tools at a level that allowed humans to dominate. So, what happened in the meantime? I do not know all of the answers you would get, but I know one would be "the tribe."

Banding together into groups, and then into tribes, is one of the most important aspects of human survival in ancient times. Without it, we would be nowhere—perhaps even extinct. The group dynamic is so ingrained in us that it prevails even to this day; ask any ostracized high school student.

Remaining in the group is hard wired into us all. There is a psychological degree of survival mode in it. In man's early development, getting cut loose from the tribe almost certainly meant death. A lone person could not survive alone for long. Even today in the modern world, people who are part of groups are better balanced emotionally and psychologically than those who are constant loners.

We have a desire to be part of the whole. We are driven to remain part of the tribe, regardless of the type of tribe, and when we are driven out, it is, if not damaging, at least irksome.

The black community as a whole is a tribe. That tribe belongs to the political tribe of the Democrats. If a black person, such as myself, leaves the Democratic tribe, we are ostracized from the black tribe. We are considered traitors.

Being a conservative, who is black, is not for the faint hearted. You must have strength of character, emotional fortitude, and conviction. If you are missing even one of these traits, you will wilt like a flower in the desert heat.

Black conservatives are considered sell-outs. We are accused of trying to be white in order to be liked, which is odd given that not all white people are conservative. The terms "Uncle Tom, coon, Oreo, token, and sell-out" are insults that become familiar. My use of the word, "and" is no accident. Black conservatives are not given an either-or with any of the terms listed. We will be called by each term at some point, and multiple times. I have been accused more than once of "self-hatred." A popular line is, "You know you're black, right?" This comment is even richer when delivered by a white person.

What is the reason for the vitriol? How can friends and associates attack you as viciously as someone who does not know you, or even a racist person? It all stems from what I explained in the last chapter. The black community has determined, come hell or high water, that the Democrat party cares for black people. They are the ones fighting for our equality, economic status, and social betterment. Their policies are best for the black community, and therefore if you are against what they stand for, then you are against your own people. It is that plain and simple. It is that black or white.

What many liberals believe is that as a conservative, I must have forgotten my roots; i.e., that I'm black. All the black conservatives in media have no convictions—they are just selling out to white people for money. If we are convinced, then it is because we have been brainwashed by someone. The disease of white supremacy has infected our souls and stolen our identity.

That is the life of a black conservative.

There are times when this cycle is emotionally damaging. I don't care how independent someone is—no one likes to be cut off from the tribe. In my own life, my friends and associates know I'm no idiot. I read more than all of them combined. So, when I say it pisses me off that any of them would assert I'm just being a sellout, rather than having given something some forethought, I'm being understated. It infuriates me.

The desire to curse them out is strong. The decision to not temper my response to them is an easy one to make. Walking them through just why they are the ones who are clueless, in exacting detail, usually by pointing out how little they pay attention to world events, is a road I have taken more than once.

In my book, Commander-in-Failure, I detail numerous examples of how I have lost and dismissed the friendships of others, because of my decision to not support Barack Obama. I doubt very much that my story is any different than other black conservative's. If I posted a question on my Facebook page, I doubt it would take me an hour to get a hundred-plus responses. By week's end, the thread would probably number close to a thousand responses.

Fortunately, my negative response towards the insults and attitudes aimed at me only accounts for maybe twenty percent of my mental space on this issue. The rest of my time is spent in bewilderment and bemusement.

When you decide to become a conservative, especially as a black person, you are freed from the chains of emotionality and cultural hegemony; better known as groupthink. You begin to see the world through the lens of logic.

When a black conservative is accused of trying to be white, the implication being made is that only a white person would be a conservative or Republican. But, of course, not all white people are Republicans. Even when you factor in the difference in population between whites and blacks, there are more whites who are Democrats than blacks. So, why aren't black Democrats "trying to be white?"

Think about it. Democrats preach the doctrine of being taken care of by and through government programs. How is that any different than being taken care of by the plantation owner? The number of white people on welfare is higher than the number of blacks, yet black Democrats fight for these programs all day long. That sounds a lot like wanting to be white to me.

The definition of a sellout is someone who has forgotten their roots. Okay, well the roots of African-Americans are Republicans. The roots of the black community are in the Christian church, where marriage, fatherhood, and life is extolled. In the black church, gay marriage was not acceptable. Homosexuality was seen as a sin, not something to be supported. Those are the roots of the black community.

In 1965, before the shift of the black community toward Democrats, 76.4 of black children were born to married women. Today it is the opposite; 70% of black children are born out of wedlock. In the sixties, 70 percent of blacks were married[20]. Today

---

20 http://www.americanthinker.com/articles/2014/03/the_decline_of_the_africanamerican_family.html

that number is 29%.[21] Pre-1973, the idea of a mother taking the life of her baby was offensive. Yes, back-alley abortions happened. But no one celebrated an abortion with cries of joy and pink bras swinging in the air—not in the white community, and not in the black community. Today, black women make up 14% of the female population in the U.S., but have 30% of the abortions. Whatever anyone thinks of homosexuality, the Bible is clear on it. It is a sin. The act of same-sex love is not affirmed in any portion of the Bible, but today most black churches support it. Today, if you go to a national meeting of the NAACP, a large portion of their agenda is dedicated to gay social and political issues. But, every evening there will be a church service.

Those are the roots of the black community. Republicans do not support gay marriage or abortion, and they hold up marriage as the ideal. Many Democrats believe abortion is perfectly fine, that marriage is not the best choice, just one choice. They prefer the state takes care of children, not fathers, and gay marriage and homosexuality are celebrated and seen as normal. If your roots—what your "tribe" believes, today and in the past—are what the Republicans believe today, but you support Democrats who don't support your historical values, then who has really forgotten where they have come from? See, my fellow blacks are telling me that I've forgotten my roots, but my roots and their roots (and yours, if you're African-American) are the values presented by the Republican party, not Democrats.

The incongruity goes further. It is one thing to talk about our historical values, but what about today? Does it not make sense to support the team that shares the values you have now? Yes, that does make sense. So, let's go on down the line.

The black community is predominantly a Christian church-going and - believing community. The Christian belief on gay

---

21 http://blackdemographics.com/households/marriage-in-black-america/

marriage is clear–it is not appropriate. Most Republicans follow that value; most Democrats do not.

Blacks cannot stand paying taxes. Trust me, I'm black, most of my friends in life have been black, none are looking for higher tax rates on themselves. Republicans nearly always fight for a lower tax rate on all citizens. Sure, you can find a few instances where tax rates were raised or new taxes were added. Usually that was because of a deal they needed to make, like when Ronald Reagan was President. Other times it was not, like when the first President Bush said, "Read my lips—no new taxes," and then broke that promise. Republicans made him pay for it at the ballot box. Democrats, on the other hand, are always fighting for higher taxes, especially on society's most successful people. If you become financially successful, you can basically count on Democrats giving you the line, "We're going to ask the rich to pay just a little bit more," as your reward. When a little bit more is always more than the last time they asked, it's not a little bit anymore. The key point, though, is if you ask a black person if they want their taxes to go up, you will get an answer in the negative, 99.8% of the time.

Despite the heartbreaking statistics on abortion within the black community, it is still frowned upon by most blacks; partly due to the Christian underpinnings of the black community. Republicans fight to keep unborn black babies alive, Democrats do not.

I have yet to ever meet a black person who does not have a side hustle—a way to make money on the side, a part-time business they are running, or thinking of running. Entrepreneurship is in our DNA. Republicans support policies that make it easier to start small businesses, Democrats support policies that make it harder to do so.

So, who is ignoring their roots and current values?

It is not me, my friend.

You can decide to believe what you want, but the Democrat party and its policies are the exact opposite of every value espoused in the church, especially the black church. Yet every Sunday, millions of black preachers and pastors support the values of the Democrat party.

Another definition of the term sell-out is dropping your principles for economic gain. The Reverend (I use that term loosely) Jesse Jackson is worth ten million dollars today. He has not garnered that money as a businessman, but as a social activist. Most of his net worth has been built in the 80s, 90s and beyond. In 1973, after the decision of Roe vs. Wade, Jackson fought against the incorrect ruling. Question, do you think Jackson is a pro-life proponent? Did you even know he fought against the ruling at one time? I bet not, because he is a reliable liberal now. If asked today, he supports a woman's right to choose to kill her baby. He has no problem with homosexuality or gay marriage. Do you think he would take a hit if he opposed both? Of course, he would.

Today he could probably recover in the public eye. But, if he had maintained his stance, per his pastoral Christian values, it is doubtful he would have made the money he has made in life.

Neither Jesse Jackson nor his contemporary Al Sharpton are seen as a religious authority figures any longer. TD Jakes is one of many black pastors who does have that title. TD Jakes has a net worth of 147 million.

ONE HUNDRED FORTY-SEVEN MILLION!

That is on par with a businessman, and in fairness, that is what he has become. He has melded the worlds of faith with business— producing movies, a television show, internet properties, and publishing. I do not begrudge him that financial success. He is not taking it from the collection plate, and he certainly comes by it more honestly than either Jackson or Sharpton. BUT...but... in 2016, Bishop Jakes answered a question about homosexuality thusly,

"...his thinking on homosexuality is 'evolved and evolving' and that it is "absolutely" possible for the gay community and the black church to coexist[22]."

Look, I'm not making an argument here about the rightness or wrongness of gay life choices. That is a separate discussion and book. My point here is that the honorific "Reverend" or "Bishop" are religious titles confirmed onto someone who has studied and teaches a definitive set of values. It is the job of a pastor to preach every Sunday, and live their lives every day according to the values of the Bible. The Bible says homosexuality is a sin. No different from committing adultery. Now maybe you believe that and maybe you don't, not the point. The point is if your doctrine teaches that belief, it is your duty to teach that belief. I find it interesting that when confronted with a simple question, that if it were answered correctly, it would affect the finances of the pastor or church; somehow these black pastors sound like liberals.

If that is not selling out, then tell me what is?

The bottom-line, underlying theme is that if you are not supporting the betterment of your group, of your tribe, then you are not for your people. And you know what, that sentiment is correct. The issue is what is bettering your people? Fully a third of the black population in American has been killed off in abortion clinics across the country. How in the name of Jesus is that a betterment of the black community? Before social welfare programs, black families were the norm; now they are not. If you are black, and a child, then there is a 70% chance you are not living in a home where Daddy comes home at night. Liberal welfare policies made that a reality in the 70s, when as a matter of policy, homes with a man living within it were denied welfare payments. The solution was an easy one—the women kicked the unmarried fathers of their kids out

22 http://www.rightwingwatch.org/post/religious-right-freaks-out-about-td-jakes-comments-on-gay-rights-church-state-separation/

of the house. The social pressure to provide for your kids was also absent, because as these men saw it, "she getting all that money from the government, she don't need none of mine." Fast-forward a few decades, and having "baby daddies" rather than fathers is now the norm. This is not the only reason for that cultural shift, but it is one of the pillars to it. But the question is—are blacks better off after the implementation of those programs and policies?

I believe that we, as blacks, can each stand on our own two feet and become successful without government and in spite of any racism. Black Democrats will also say that the black community can stand on its own two feet, and then argue for more money in CHIP, welfare, housing, and child care. Yet, as discussed, all the programs they have gotten have not made people self-sufficient. Tell me, is someone better off on welfare and government assistance, or better off taking care of themselves with a job and career?

I want what is best for people who look like me. I want that because they are black and because they are Americans. I want them to excel, and for them to do that as a people, they cannot be Democrats. That makes me, and all the black conservatives like me, more caring about our people than everyone who is calling us Uncle Toms.

Blacks who are conservative and live their lives according to their beliefs have better lives than Democrats. That is right. If you are black and follow the tenets of liberalism, as it pertains to blacks in America, then your life probably sucks. You are more likely to be on public assistance, living in a small ghetto apartment or project, with few job prospects.

I can hear the words now— "That is ridiculous. There are millions of blacks who have jobs, good lives, wealth, etc., and are Democrats. Most are, in fact, Democrats."

That would be correct, but they are not living their lives like liberals. They did not stay home and whine about education—

they went out and got their degrees. They go to work every day. They work hard; some even save money. Many get married and raise their kids as a married family. Others do not stop being responsible just because a man is not around. They do what is necessary to try and give their children a good life.

Those attitudes are all Republican ones. They are attitudes of action and creativity. They are affirmations of "I have to make this happen. Me, not Uncle Sam." Liberal thought is not like that. The liberal action is inaction. It is worrying about racism all the time, even when it is not present. Liberalism seeks to make you believe that what others have keeps you from having it. Liberalism stresses the masses over your individual choice. People who follow those tenets in their life are not successful. Those who preach them, like Bernie Sanders, Elizabeth Warren, or Barack Obama, sure seem to use the system they hate to sell their books, buy their big homes, and get out of taxes.

That is the big irony of the black community. They accuse me of being an Uncle Tom for supporting the mindset and values of Republicans, but most still live their lives like one every day. They act like Republicans until the subject of politics comes up, or it is time to vote. They walk into the voting booth Red, then turn Blue and vote against themselves.

When 90% of the black community votes Democrat, "all down the line," they are voting against their own best interests, against many of the values they still practice and are the ones that are voting in a manner consistent with insults of "Uncle Tom, sell-out, or brainwashed."

Think on this. When slavery was the norm in America, Democrats supported it. They fought a war to keep it. They housed their slaves in quarters that were squalid. Today, blacks support the party that supported slavery. They support the party that founded the KKK and used the group to terrorize blacks. They support the party whose policies and "social" programs keep many blacks living in the ghettos. Would you not call those areas squalid, at least in modern terms, as well?

I loathe those who tell me that I cannot think for myself, and that I must support a political party with that history and with the modern results I see today. I despise any who tell me that supporting a party that fights for the right of every child, born or unborn, black or white to live, is me being a "coon." I chuckle in derision at those who get hot under the collar when someone acts like they like watermelon "just because they are black," and then tell me, "Don't you remember you are black? Vote Democrat."

I'm no one's Uncle anything. Neither is any other black conservative.

We are the people with the highest degree of courage within the black community. We were strong enough to walk away from the tribe because we can see clearly the tribe is being led off a cliff.

CHAPTER 10
Discouragement... Not Inspiration

One of the biggest public debates in the country right now is illegal immigration. We have around 11 million people here illegally. We do not know who these people are. Many, around two million of them, are projected to be members of gangs, like MS-13. They broke the law to get into this country, making a mockery of the people who come to the U.S. legally.

Despite that fact, Democrats call these people "undocumented immigrants" or "undocumented Americans" and fight to keep them here. There are some Democrats who have no desire to make the flow into the country a legal and orderly affair. They wish for open borders, and to make it easier for the people who snuck here to become legal citizens.

Anyone who wants them to go home first, or deport them, is called a racist. If you prefer to reward the people who filled out an I-485 form (the government form for legal residence for immigrants) first, then you are anti-immigrant. The rhetoric and name-calling fall fast and furious from the Democrats on this issue.

I find it fascinating for reasons not connected to the issues of immigration at all. We have an organized campaign, legally, socially, electorally, and in the media, to fight for the right of someone who snuck into American through a hole in the ground to stay here. But every day, we hear from those same Democrats about how racist, horrible, hateful, and lacking in opportunity America is.

I'm sorry, but if America is all those things, if we are filled with an animus against others, if we lack in opportunity for all people, then why do you want these poor souls to be here? More importantly, if that is how our country is, then why are Mexicans coming through the deserts, under the ground in tunnels, and placing themselves or family into a blood debt to drug cartels for a Coyote to guide them past U.S. Border patrol? Why are Asians willing to make the same deal with the Chinese Triad, and Japanese Yakuza, just to be crammed into shipping containers, and snuck into the country? Why are Haitians stringing together three logs and calling it a boat to come to America? Why do thousands of people from dozens of countries come to the United States, legally, every year?

Do you see the malfunction here? On the one hand, Democrats are campaigning on the idea that America is no longer the land of opportunity, or that it is still a racist country. On the other hand, they are fighting for these people to stay here, and to make it easier for more people to come.

You cannot have it both ways. Either America is a beacon of hope and opportunity, or we are racist, hateful, and lacking opportunity.

But this is exactly the case with the Democrat party. At every level, they have ideas, speeches, and attitudes that convey how some groups cannot get the American dream—and only because of what they look like.

It does not matter what level of life you are discussing. You could be talking about the country as President, senator, locally elected official, sports coach, CEO, business owner, or pastor, but when people decide to follow you, they want to be inspired. We wish to see the possibilities in life. Yes, we know there are obstacles;

that is a part of life. But, we want to know we can overcome them. We want to know they can be overcome.

That is not a feeling I get from any leader in the Democrat side of life. Let us take the most popular one, Barack Obama. President Obama gave a lot of economic speeches in his tenure as Commander in Chief. No one remembers all the speeches, but we do remember the best phrases, golden hits like:

"Everyone needs to pay a fair share so that everyone can have a fair shot."—State of Union Speech.

"If you got a business, you didn't build that."—Campaign 2012 Speech

"We have by no means, overcome the legacies of slavery and Jim Crow and colonialism and slavery."—Daily Show Dec 12, 2016

And my personal favorite, an excerpt from an upcoming book about President Obama's past, written by a liberal and socialist sympathizer, David Garrow, from an earlier book Obama and a friend began writing. The excerpt reads like this:

America is an admittedly racist nation. We cannot realistically expect White America to make special concessions toward blacks over the long haul. The greatest testimony to the force of racist ideology in American culture is that it infects not only the mind of whites, but the mind of blacks as well."

Rising Star, The Making of Barack Obama

He goes on to write that social reforms needed to address the race issue must be snuck by to be implemented.

Obama is not alone in his sentiments. A casual viewing of MSNBC will show you, within an hour, at least two or more people, often one of the hosts, taking about the evils of our country. Not the evils of the past, which are real, but the evils of the present. You will hear from people like Van Jones of CNN, how blacks are getting screwed, how women are getting screwed, or of course how the immigrants who fled their countries are going to get screwed.

But it's ok. There is a solution. In order for the opportunity for all reality to come true, we just have to institute Democratic, liberal social reforms. If we increase our taxes on wealthy Americans, then your child has a shot at a good school and the American dream. If we just strengthen our racial quotas or racially-based social programs, black children can get a piece of prosperity. Just give everyone free college, free universal pre-K (because you know preschool determines your kid's whole life), free health care; free, free, and freer. That is the answer.

If you are not personally into those ideas or don't think they will work, then obviously, you wish the "other" ill will.

It is not just the blacks and minorities, either. Bernie Sanders and Elizabeth Warren can tell you all about how corporations are the bane of American society. One quote from his presidential campaign is *"The billionaires of America are on the warpath. They want more and more and more."* He has made a career out of attacking the rich and corporations. It is little wonder that his followers do not want to work. Who wants to work for an evil corporation that screws over their workers? Who would want to be complicit in a company that is destroying the environment or poisoning Americans everyday just for *money?* How could anyone stand for a company that pays their well-educated CEO millions of dollars, when the janitor is just scraping by with ten dollars an hour? After listening to one speech of his, I would not want to work there either.

And yet, the people come—Asians, Africans, Mexicans, Muslims, Indians, South Americans—they continue to come to the US. They flock to our shores like ants to sugar. They arrive, often with little money and no English skills, and make a life for themselves. They become business owners and homeowners. They make sure their kids do well in school and take advantage of an apparent opportunity that does not seem to exist to Democrats.

I understand stomping out racism, sexism, corruption, and corporate greed when they rear their evil heads. Everyone must be given an equal opportunity. However, it is incorrect to act like that is not the norm.

I get sick of hearing from my "leaders" that because I'm black, I cannot do something. No, I want every senator and congressman to sound like a damned motivational speaker. Don't tell me, Mr. Obama, how I or other young black kids cannot get a fair shake as a black person. Talk to us about how a black man with a funny name that rhymes with Osama became President, and how that shows America is not the country it was 100 years ago.

I've been black for 35-plus years. I have never been whipped, denied service, went into a "black only" section, or attacked by the KKK. I've been to college and gotten educated. I've had white men choose me for promotions over other white men.

I can turn on the television and see blacks headlining news programs. I see black billionaires and millionaires. I drive by blacks every day with homes and expensive cars. I see blacks who are living the American dream. To act and speak as if it is impossible is beyond silly. It is stupid.

Now it is fair to ask, "Is it enough?" Are the economics for blacks or minorities where they should be? Assuming we could all agree on what that number is, it is fair to say no. As related in past chapters, the general income gap between blacks and whites is large. The wealth difference is even larger.

Yet when you look at black people not born in America—groups like Nigerians for example—they are being educated at high levels. The same is true for blacks from the West Indies. In fact, black immigrants earn 30% more than native-born blacks[23].

Racism should make that impossible. If a white person dislikes blacks, they do not make exceptions for an immigrant who is

23 http://www.blackenterprise.com/money/black-immigrants-in-u-s-earning-30-more-than-u-s-born-blacks/

likely darker, has an accent, and a name they cannot pronounce. If anything, they would dislike them more.

Let me ask you a question, and if you do not know the answer, consider it a homework assignment. How many strip malls have you driven past that housed a nail salon owned by someone from Asia? They could be Korean, Vietnamese, or Chinese. If you drive by six strip malls, I bet you drive by six nail shops, all owned by Asians.

In the black community, there are few things more important than a black woman's hair. Weaves, hair extensions, and hair products are an industry that would frankly collapse if black women stopped buying products for one month. But, when you walk into these shops, they are owned by Indians, Pakistanis, or Koreans.

How many jokes are there about 7-11s and Indian owners?

These are not derogatory stereotypes. They are examples of specific cash-generating business enterprises that immigrants have come to dominate. Their customers are the same people who certain leaders in blue, think cannot succeed because of barriers in the country.

Why and how are these immigrants doing it, then? Explain to me how the opportunity of America is the birthright of every person born here, but some natives of America, i.e. minorities, are not taking advantage of the opportunity?

I could be wrong. I am sure there are a lot of reasons, but one I will just slap down on the list is that *certain politicians, leaders, and political groups keep telling these people that there is no opportunity for them.* It saddens me to look at this great county and see examples of all types of people prospering, perhaps not rich, but doing well, and never hear about it from Democrats.

Nothing in life needs to be perfect for it to be excellent. Millions of people would not flock to this country if there were not an opportunity available. If they were going to be massively oppressed here, believe me, the word would get out, and people would not come. Do you think Sandi Arabia has the illegal immigration problem that America has? Does it even have the legal immigration numbers we have? What about China? Are people flocking from England, the Middle East, and Japan to move there? Is there any group jumping into boats in the sea to reach North Korea?

No, no, and no. "*They are coming to America*," as the words in Neil Diamond's song says.

No one gets the American dream without a business or a job. Who provides the jobs in America? Corporations provide those jobs. Wal-Mart employs two million people, but Democrats demonize them. The superstore giant allows low-income people to buy more items they need at lower prices than before Wal-Mart became a national brand. But Wal-Mart is the devil.

Insurance companies are moneygrubbers, according to Elizabeth Warren, but how many insurance claims has she paid out? How many jobs has she created with her anti-capitalist rhetoric? The insurance industry employees 2.5 million Americans. They pay out billions in claims each year.

I get depressed listening to Democrats attack the institutions that we need, realizing that without them, America would disappear overnight. Our country cannot function without corporations. If we waved corporations and the tax money they provide away tomorrow, we really would have no opportunity. We would turn into less than a third world country.

I sit back and at times and ask myself, "What in the world is the Democrats' freakin malfunction?"

I do not want to hear how all corporations are screwing everyone over. I want to hear about the good corporations who provide a decent example of how success in America occurs. I do not want to hear about how every white person, not a Democrat, hates me. I have no desire to listen to another speech about the lack of opportunity for me because I am black. I want to hear how racism cannot hold me back because America is not the nation it used to be.

I want to hear the damned truth. And the truth is that Obama, Oprah, and Condi Rice did not exist in 1940. They could not have done what they have in modern times back then. In the 1920s, there were no black congressmen. In the 1970s, you did not see blacks in professional level jobs, sporting dreadlocks.

The past does not sadden me. The past of America fills me with hope and energy because I can see where we have come as a nation. I can look back and see what my grandfather endured, and rise tomorrow knowing I will not face that. I can look back on the past when the rich truly were the same people, and the only ones getting richer, to today where most of the wealthiest people were not rich thirty years ago. I can go to the library and look at a Forbes' Richest 400 list from 1982 and compare it to today. Nearly all the top ten people from 1982 are absent on the list in 2016. Every day I can go on the internet and find stories about people starting businesses and succeeding at levels unheard of even 25 years ago.

No, the past does not sadden me. The Present Democrat party of Obama, Warren, Schumer, and Sanders saddens me. The glorious truth of America surrounds them every day, but all we hear is that nothing has changed. All I hear is not how you or I can better ourselves. We are told that we need the Democrats to ensure our future.

Imagine a cocktail party. You have two tables you can sit at for the duration of the night, and you get to sample each one first. At one table, you tell them about a business idea you are pursuing. That table encourages you, tells you can succeed, and even gives you a few ideas on how to start. Then you move to the second table and give the same information. But here, you are told that as a black, or woman, or even non-college educated white person, there is no way you will be accepted. There is too much… pick the "-ism" of your choice… for you to succeed.

Which table will you spend your night at?

When I hear Republicans speak, what I hear are the possibilities. When I hear Democrats speak, all I hear are imagined negativities and obstacles. If I want to know what I cannot do and why I just need to go to a Democrat rally, if I want to hear what is possible for me, no matter what, then I go to a Republican rally.

I love my country and myself. So I choose the Republican way.

I see what my country has become, not what it was or used to be. I now have the opportunity. The sacrifices and fights of the past have been won. I'm on the playing field, and now everything is up to me. Others have taken the ball down the field of play and scored.

I do not hear that from Democrats, and so I turn away from them.

CHAPTER 11

American Stalinism

The eight statements of principles written on the photo that went viral on my Facebook account were the original impetus for this book. This book expands on and explains the thoughts behind each of them. But I find I need to add an extra chapter. As an adult, and certainly as a freelance journalist reporting on the political issues of the Obama era, I've come to notice a darker and more malevolent problem with Democratic thought, policy, and progressive philosophy.

Democrats have come to express, fight for, and believe in an American form of Stalinism. Stalinism is the ideology and policy of a centralized government, totalitarianism, and the pursuit of communism. Totalitarianism is the belief in a system of government that is not only centralized in set up, but is dictatorial and requires complete subservience to the state, or state rules. Communism, of course, is the belief that class warfare is appropriate and necessary. All assets should be redistributed, and it should be publicly owned.

For all the "-isms" that Democrats purport to fight, and claim the Republic must be saved from, it is these "-isms"—Stalinism, totalitarianism, communism, and fascism that are the largest threats to the country.

Very few of those political movements are taught in schools today. You are not likely to encounter them until college. At universities, almost universally liberal, students are taught the romantic notion of Carl Marx (creator of the notion of communism) as a leader for the average man. They seldom point out that Marxist regimes killed over 110 million people between 1917 and 1987[24]. Joseph Stalin killed 20 million[25].

So, what are these political philosophies, and how do they match the Democrats of today?

These are the general principals:

• A central government that makes the laws for the whole country, and controls the decision-making aspects of education, economics, tax, and social policy.

• Dictatorial in its laws. The public must follow the dictates of the central government without opposition. The opposition is wiped out, usually by death or prisons.

• Either Communism or Socialism as the economic status of the country. The state owns most or a great deal of the lands, hard assets (think oil fields), or if not, taxes at a high level for funneling money into the centralized government. In exchange, a large public welfare state is established to provide "basic" services to all citizens.

24 http://www.wnd.com/2004/12/28036/
25 http://necrometrics.com/20c5m.htm#Stalin

These are the textbook general principles. In plain English, I would say they represent the belief that the government is in control of almost everything, and will tell you what to do, say, believe, and even buy.

This is what we have in all aspects of the government from Democrats. Let me show you, one by one.

America is 50 states. Each state has its own laws, regulations, and local governments. The Constitution dictated what the federal government can and cannot do. However, over the years, the reach of the federal government has grown. The push for Obamacare is one in which the government created a law that took over how the insurance industry would operate in each state. The law treats the states of Florida, California, and Idaho the same. The idea that healthcare specific to the population of each state might make more sense is dismissed.

The people who support Obamacare would say all people deserve health care coverage. Ok, fine. What is wrong with 50 different systems that provide their state citizens with healthcare? Why do we need one standard across the whole country?

"Education standards" is the catch phrase for any policy on how to treat or teach students. The Department of Education and the President can dictate what they want through force of funding. So if Texas wants to keep only boys in the boy's locker room and showers, then the Federal says, no, allow girls in the boy's locker room or showers, or lose your funding. Title 9 funding for schools is now contingent on schools having equal women and men's sports. If the school was too small for a girls' volley ball team, then too bad. They lost funding.

Democrats continually fight for more and more centralized control from DC in all aspects of American life. When they use the word "universal," it usually means both free and something that is created in Washington.

What follows the centralized attitude is the worst aspect of Democrat thinking, and what scares me most—the dictatorial attitude. See, in a country with over 320 million people, and disparate political views, there are bound to be differences in how we each view life. We are a nation of religious freedom, so the values that people live by and would like to be reflected in society differ as well.

Republicans will argue with you all day long, but will not seek to force you to believe what we believe. If you don't want to be a Christian, fine, don't go to church. Don't like guns, that is fine, don't buy one. You can leave your family unprotected, but I'm protecting mine. If you want to buy a toy car to save the planet, go ahead, I'm keeping my SUV. That is the conservative mindset. Not so for Democrats. In the Democrat world, if they believe something is bad or wrong, they move to force you into accepting what they believe. Do you think this is a hyperbolic statement ? Continue reading, and I'll prove it.

If you are Christian and do not believe in the homosexual lifestyle and gay marriage, then you must be forced into acceptance. Refuse to do business with customers who are seeking services from you in order to participate in a gay marriage ceremony, and you will be taken to court and forced to do so, or lose your business. You will be mocked and demonized on news programs, social media, and likely have a petition to boycott your business on Change.org. However, would anyone think it was appropriate sue to a black baker and force them to make a cake for a KKK rally? Umm, no.

Democrats are now threatening churches with payback if they do not perform gay marriage ceremonies. They also boycott companies or people who do not agree with gay marriage, and seek to destroy them. It is not enough for you to say, "I do not agree, but this is America, so do what you want," you must openly accept their worldview.

If you do not accept that worldview, then they try to hurt you. Sometimes that is through legal means. More often, though, it is liberals threatening businesses, trying to shut down speeches they do not like at colleges, or of course attacking you on social media. See, they exercise their free speech to attack you, but deny your own freedom of speech if you disagree with them.

That is textbook fascism. Let's look at another example.

Obesity is a problem. There are many reasons for it, but health studies have shown that trans fats are a contributing factor. And just so we're on that same page, we are talking about junk foods and prepackaged foods. Democrats decided that trans fats were not just a bad thing, but a thing they needed to stop companies and people from eating. So they wrote a law that stated companies had to get rid of trans fats in their foods. Were they causing cancer, or poisoning people? No, but it was decided that since "science" said it made people fat (even though there are more fat people today than before non-trans-fat was a thing) companies needed to be forced to take out the ingredients. Why? Trust me, no one needed a law to know potato chips were fattening.

It is now law for calories to be posted on fast food menus, as if no one knows that fast food is not healthy. Former New York city Mayor Michael Bloomberg decided that large soft drinks were unhealthy, so he decided to make a law that forced stores to stop selling certain cup sizes. Other Democrat mayors have created a sugar tax on sodas because they think sodas are making Americans fat.

We have a new president in the country, trying to do things that are perfectly legal. But liberals are suing, and liberal judges are making up laws to stop President Trump. They could not beat him at the voting booth, so they are using the courts, and creating case law that is not Constitutionally-based, or in the case of the travel ban, the same thing that President Obama did.

And it goes on.

Democrats have decided that manmade global warming is a real thing, and now if you do not agree, you are ridiculed. There are scientists at universities who have refuted the computer models regarding global warming, and who have been fired. Democrats fight for taxes on carbon emissions, even though it will make everything more expensive. President Obama and Hilary Clinton have both talked about wanting—no, needing—to put coal companies out of business for the good of the planet.

See, it is not good enough to try and convince people to follow them. You must be forced to accept, and will be punished if you do not. In 2016, the California Senate proposed a bill that would prosecute anyone who was a climate dissenter[26].

Let me put this in the opposite vein. Imagine Republicans taking you to court for not wanting a gun in your house, or for not believing in the second amendment? The idea is patently ridiculous, because Republicans would not think of doing something so stupid. But this is the norm for Democrats and progressives: use any means at their disposal to force what they want on you. Use the courts to bypass citizen-passed legislation, use social media to get people fired for not agreeing to whatever policy or social belief that want you to follow. Chip and Joanna Gaines, of HGTV fame for "Fixer Upper," were attacked by the gay lobby, just because of their church. They have not even spoken out on the issue of gay marriage themselves.

What makes this trend worse is that it is targeted. The Muslim faith is as anti-gay and anti-gay-marriage as Christians are, but you do not see mosques or Muslims being targeted. Perhaps it is because liberals know they could literally lose their heads over it.

Democrats are all for women's rights, but where is their support for the 16-year-old girl who does not want to get undressed next to a boy pretending to be a girl? Democrats scream about Republicans

26 http://www.washingtontimes.com/news/2016/jun/2/calif-bill-prose-cutes-climate-change-skeptics/

"not believing in science," but the fact of biological science stares them right in the face on the issue of transgender mental delusion, and they ignore it. Further, if you insist that a male stay in the male bathroom or locker room, you are called a bigot. The North Carolina bathroom law is couched as a discrimination issue, but where is the discrimination? A boy needs to use the bathroom, no one is keeping him from doing so; the bathroom is right there. It's called the "men's bathroom." And not to be crude, but as long as you have a penis and male DNA, you are a male. How you feel about yourself is not relevant. Or at least it should not be.

Women must be protected from the ravages of rape, and violence against them. Ok, that makes sense. Where are these Democrats on the issue of a woman's right to carry a gun? Women in the cities of DC and New York do not have that right. They cannot get a concealed-carry license in either location. Why can't these women have a gun, per their Constitutional rights, to protect themselves from getting raped? The answer is because Democrats have decided that guns are bad, and therefore no one should have them. Except, of course, the liberals who can afford private guards. Yes, the Constitution protects it, but that hardly matters, since they keep appointing judges who do not accept the constitution as it is written. No, they have this philosophy of a "living Constitution," whose words and meanings change as society changes.

A few years ago, the technology and cost for a rearview camera in a car finally aligned to the point of affordability. Car companies could not offer it as an option to buyers and still make money on the car. It is a great idea, but hardly necessary for safe driving. Nonetheless, rearview cameras will soon be required in all cars by law.

Why should you or I be forced to have a car that will be more expensive because of this requirement? The answer is because some Democrat lawmakers decided it was a good idea, and therefore everyone must have them. Well, I don't need one. I've been driving and backing up just fine without a camera for thirty years.

I can say this many ways, with dozens of examples, but the concept is simple. Democrats do not want a democracy. They want a "democracy" that allows them to dictate what everyone must do. They wish to *force* you to do what they want you to do. That is totalitarianism; that is fascism.

Now, maybe you're a Democrat who is reading this and is thinking, "I don't want to do any of that. I don't want to force people to do things." Maybe *you* do not. But what do you make of what I've laid out so far? See, the Democrats fighting the bathroom law in North Carolina are forcing a girl to be in a state of undress next to a boy or man. They are trying to normalize the idea that your granddaughter in high school should have no qualms about showering with a boy who thinks he's a girl. That's your party's policy. It's your party's policy to take the healthy diet decisions a person should make out of their hands by force of law. As I alluded to before, there are more fat people today, after trans-fat laws, than before them. So clearly, they are not the reason people are fat or unhealthy.

At some point, you have to divorce yourself away from what you think personally and ask yourself, "what am I supporting with my vote?"

In 2013, Democrat Congressman Keith Ellison spoke to a reporter about his "Inclusive Prosperity Act" which proposed government programs on health care, climate change mitigation efforts, and adaption efforts abroad. He said the new programs would be paid for with new taxes. *"The bottom line is, we're [the U.S. government] not broke, there's plenty of money; it's just the government doesn't have it[27]."*

---

27 http://www.cnsnews.com/news/article/rep-ellison-there-s-plenty-money-it-s-just-government-doesn-t-have-it

Where do you think the money that the government does not have is located? It is in your pockets and mine. It is the money in the pockets of the American people, but Ellison believes the government should have access to it—not the people who worked for it, but the government, so they can spend it on the people who did not work for it—including, apparently, foreigners.

Democrat Congresswoman Maxine Waters has said in the past that private oil fields are the American public's resources and property, not the oil companies. Despite her silly statement, Democrats have not *quite* moved to the idea of taking all assets under the government arm. Communism is not on their agenda—yet.

But Democrats, in policy, if not in talk, do fight for a more socialistic economic system. In general, Democrats do not like "the one percent." They believe that the one percent are stealing from the regular folks, do not pay their fair share of taxes, and have too much money in their hands.

The simple fact that few people in the one percent were born with it, or that 90% of the millionaires in the country got that money by working for it, is not relevant. Just like Stalin, Mao, and Marx, they wrap their dislike in the moral cloak of helping "the people," but the truth is, they just need to pay for their centralized government.

When you have a large central government, you need money to make it run. If the government is only in charge of a few things, then you do not need as much tax revenue. However, if you are going to take over everything, then you need the resources to feed it. That is why all socialist countries and centralized governments lead to high taxation, and eventually totalitarianism rule. You need the money, and you must force the people to give it to you.

I'm a grown-ass man, perfectly capable of getting a job. Why would I need the government to pay for my health insurance?

What do we need universal pre-K for? The admittance of a four-year-old into pre-k of any kind has no effect, positive or negative, on their future life prospects. I barely remember kindergarten, let alone preschool. Democrats in the health and human services department during Obama's term began a program called Connect that allows the inner-city low-income families to have free internet access. Why is that even necessary? It is a vital role of the government to provide that to citizens. Wouldn't those families be better off with a job that allows them to buy their own internet service? Of course it would.

There is a long-established rule that social entitlements, once established, are difficult to stop. Once Americans get used to getting something from the government, then they don't want it taken away. They come to believe they are owed it—that they are entitled to it—hence the term "entitlements."

This human response is how you control the population. Take Obamacare, for example. Whatever your opinion of the law, it is under no dispute that the costs are going higher than expected. People cannot afford it or the deductibles. Nonetheless, Democrats fight to make sure it does not get taken away. Think about it. You have something that does not work for you and you cannot afford, but you fight to keep it around.

When people do that in marriage, we send them to therapy.

That is the natural pathway of central governments and how they seek to stay in power. The problem is not just Democratic politicians. Half of American voters vote Democratic, and they want these policies.

They want more government control of our lives. They see the government as a force for good. They, therefore, have no problem with, for the supposed good of the citizens, forcing you to believe what they believe. You must believe that if a boy sees himself as a girl, it does not matter if he has a penis and scrotum, she is a girl. It is perfectly legal to force you to buy health insurance with the benefits they tell you to have, because someone in the central government knows what you, living in Arizona, need to have. It is justifiable to take your ranch land away when heavy rain creates a pond because it is now a wetland[28].

That is Stalinism. That is totalitarianism. That is a dictatorship. And that, my friend, is scary.

I will not be part of the collective. I will not be assimilated like a victim of the Borg[29]. America was founded on the ideals of self-determination, freedom, and the rights of the individual being separate and in ways more important than the governments. Freedom means I'm free to believe what religion I want, where I want to live, what I want to buy or not buy, and what I want to believe.

I do not have to believe in gay marriage. I do not need to accept abortion as moral. I do not have to accept climate change. I have a right to buy a gas-guzzler if I want. I have these freedoms because freedom is a God-given right. And you, if you choose to, can think God is a mythical story created by men. You are free to do that.

Republicans are happy to let you think that if you want. Democrats are happy to force me into accepting that God does not exist, or anything else they want me to believe. And that is why I am not a Democrat.

28 http://www.washingtontimes.com/news/2015/aug/30/andy-johnson-wyoming-farmer-sues-epa-over-16m-fine/
29 https://en.wikipedia.org/wiki/Borg_(Star_Trek)

EPILOGUE

Natural Born Conservative is more than just a book that seeks to answer the question *Why I, Kiara Ashanti, am a conservative and Republican.* It is also an opus—if you will permit me a second of aggrandizement—a manifesto on many of the things I find objectionable about Democrats. If you happened to be a Democrat, then it may be that last part, "Democrats," you have a small problem with. It is entirely possible for you to have read this book and decided that the things I ascribe to Democrats do not fit, because you do not think in those ways. Perhaps you are a business owner and therefore do not hate or disparage the rich business owner. There are Democrats who do not accept abortion as a proxy for birth control. Maybe, just maybe you agree with me on a great deal in this book, and your response is "Kiara, not all Democrats are like that. You are generalizing."

It is an accusation I have heard from the small amount of friends who have bothered to try and understand my choice. And you are correct, I am generalizing. I do not apologize for that. The reason is that when talking about social policy, politics, or even male-female dynamics, when you look at things from the macro, you are talking about what happens most of the time.

Generalities or even stereotypes are general attributes that people will encounter from the chosen group of discussion, most of the time. A common generalization about blacks is that all black people can dance. That, of course, is false. Not *every* black person can dance. Nonetheless, most black people do have rhythm and can dance. A person thinking or saying "black people are such great dancers" does not make them wrong. Generally speaking, it is true. The only issue is when you refuse to acknowledge the exception, when you are confronted with one.

Generalizations exist because we cannot try and account for every single possible exception to a rule or situation. Generalities exist because there are norms and percentages that dictate them.

I have used a broad brush with the use of "Democrats," "Republicans," and "Liberals" because it is easier to write. The fact that there are people who consider themselves Democrats, but do not agree with, say, Elizabeth Warren, is obvious to me. I think it should be to anyone else reading this or any other book.

Look, this book is about an exception to a rule: blacks are Democrats. Now, I'm black and I'm not a Democrat. I do not begrudge anyone, however, making a generalization about blacks and their voting habits, because 90% of the black community does vote Democratic. I repeat—there are exceptions in life for everything, but they are not the rule. A single Democrat's personal aversion to abortion does not erase the party's platform on it. Their personal opposition to abortion is not reflected in Democrat party platforms, legislation, or even most commentary in cable news. What you hear is a support for "health care rights" and a desire to expand the availability to abortions. Thus, I feel it is appropriate to say that Democrats support abortion.

If you are a Democrat, and the boxes I have presented here in terms of what is conservative versus liberal, or Republican versus Democrat, do not match up with your personal view, then you may want to consider three possibilities. One, you may consider yourself a Democrat because that is what you vote for, but your values are not aligned with the Democrat party. This is the heart of the manner for the few friends who have talked to me about this issue. Many of the reasons I give for being a conservative, they agree with me about. The unspoken question is usually, "So why can you be a Democrat, since we agree on that?" What they do not realize is they are voting Democrat out of habit, but not from their life values. Their life values are the opposite of the Democrat platform, but they continue to vote blue anyway. If you found yourself agreeing with me often here, then that is a signal that the platform of the Democrats is not who you are.

Two, you may be getting caught between two things—what you believe, and not liking the Republican candidate. What makes politics hard is that policies do not run for office, people do. There are a lot of people on either side who run for office who are just plain assholes. Talking to you, Harry Reid! Or they say stupid stuff; have you heard about a guy named Todd Atkin? Or worse, are plain creepy; Anthony Weiner, need I say more? When the policy or party values are being spoken by someone you do not like, it takes a great deal of character and fortitude to vote for the policy, and ignore the person. The 2016 presidential election is a prime example of this personal pickle. If you are a person who has always voted Democrat in the past, and are now coming to realize that your personal values were not aligned with the Democrat platform, it was still a long shot for you to switch, when you had Donald Trump as the presidential candidate.

Three, the person is not the platform. I'm sure I can find exceptions to everything I have written as the Democrat beliefs; ditto for Republicans. But what you believe is not what the party believes. Everything single thing I have written about Democrats is true in the macro sense, and definitively true in terms of their platform. If you are a Democrat who believes in the second amendment, does not like abortion, is not seeking to live off the government, and thinks people should not do so either, and you celebrate the business success of those who have created businesses that have made them immensely rich, then you may be one of those Democrats who has been left behind by your party. The Democrats of the 60s under Kennedy is not the party that is being run by Nancy Pelosi, Chuck Schumer, and Elizabeth Warren. The Democrat party today is a progressive group. Progressives want the state to control and take care of people, they want large centralized governments, they think emotion is more important than reality, and they revel in identity politics. If none of that sounds like you, the issue is not me generalizing about Democrats. It's that you no longer have a party—and have not realized it yet.

If I woke up tomorrow and the Republicans were fighting for policies that are the opposite of the values I have listed in this book, I would not be Republican any more. Because of my background, it is easier for me to do that, than I think others, especially black Democrats. This brings me to the question, "Could I ever vote for a Democrat?"

Well, the correct question is not could I ever, it is could I ever *again*. I have voted for a Democrat in the past. In college, when I was not as tuned into what the moral underpinnings of politics and policy needed to be, I voted for Bill Clinton when he ran for reelection. My reasoning was simple. He had turned things around, he embraced policies that worked, and so he deserved to be reelected.

Today I am older, and wiser. I understand that the philosophy and moral underpinnings of a political view will form the policies that a politician will support. Thus, it's not likely that I would ever vote for a Democrat again. Not because I am stubborn or blind, as I say rank-and-file Democrats are, but because of the policy. See, show me a Democrat who is for gun rights, against abortion, and not interested in socialistic economics, *and* is willing to fight policies that support those things; I could get behind a person like that. Unfortunately, there is no one in Democratic politics that is like that. Even if they say it personally, like Joe Manchin of West Virginia has at times, they ultimately take one for the team and support those policies.

But what about you? If you are on the blue side of the aisle, but feel like my description of Democrat beliefs are not what you believe, then when are you going to make the switch? If you believe innocent life has a right to be born, there is a party that fights for that. If you want to able to defend yourself in your home or car with your guaranteed right to a gun… there *is* a party that fights for that. If you believe that opportunity is available to all who are willing to work for it, then there is a party that believes that as well.

Their color of choice just happens to be red. It might be time for you to consider moving over to our team.

AFTERWORD

My name is Kiara Ashanti. I'm a black man in America, and I'm a conservative. I am a Republican. I make no apologies for being either. I'm not brainwashed. My head is clear. My moral compass points to true north.

The question is not why I am a Republican or conservative. The question is, why aren't you? Why are you not standing up for the rights of the human unborn? Why are you ok with the government attempting to take more and more of your money? Why, if you are black, are you supporting the party that keeps abortion clinics in our cities and not jobs? Why support the party of Jim Crow, the Ku Klux Klan, and segregationists?

The insults of "coon, Uncle Tom, Tom-boy, and sell-out" may annoy me, but they do not deter me. I know I am right, and the Democrats wrong. I can see the evidence of it all around me. I have laid it all bare in this book. In truth, I could write another two hundred pages on it. There are dozens of books that confirm my own experiences.

Perhaps a white person can afford to be a Democrat. Maybe in the grand scheme of things, if you are inclined to view the world through a racial lens, it makes no difference for the white community which party they affiliate to. But, I am black.

I am black and proud to be black. I care about my community. I care enough to see the devastation of liberal policies on my people and turn from the people who promote them. If I want to see the truth of Democratic rule, all I need to do is walk through my grandmother's hometown in Camden, New Jersey. The proof of the effectiveness of liberal policies is in every cracked street corner, dilapidated building, poor school rating, and aimless black youth in the streets.

A clear-minded African-American is morally incapable of being a Democrat. Unfortunately, too many of my brothers and sisters are not clear-headed. Cultural hegemony and internal social norms have put them into a fugue state of mind. They can neither see nor accept the devastation around them. All they can hear are the words, "We care." I'm sorry to say, they follow Democrats as doggedly as the Walkers on the Walking Dead—they follow the noise.

I'm also happy to say that it is changing. Go on to Twitter, Facebook, and Instagram. The number of blacks escaping the Democratic mental plantation is growing. There is a quiet but steady revolution growing within the black community. Conservatism is growing and expanding. Will it grow fast enough to make the Democrats take notice, and alter their… solutions? I do not know.

But if it continues to grow, the problems of the black community will begin to diminish. You see, once you start to believe and think like a conservative, you do not wait for the government to save you. You decide to save yourself. You decide to save your community despite the government.

It starts with one person and grows to millions. The Jewish people were once hated in this country and had very little. One by one, they built themselves up, and then their community up. Now, they are an economical and political force to be reckoned with. The Irish did the same. As did the Spanish communities. Blacks are a little late to the party, but I read social media, and it gives me hope.

You know why I am a conservative, but one day you won't be so surprised when meeting another black conservative. I believe that wholeheartedly, and when it happens, it will be a glorious day.

Kiara Ashanti, the Dreadlocked Republican. @dredlockedrepub

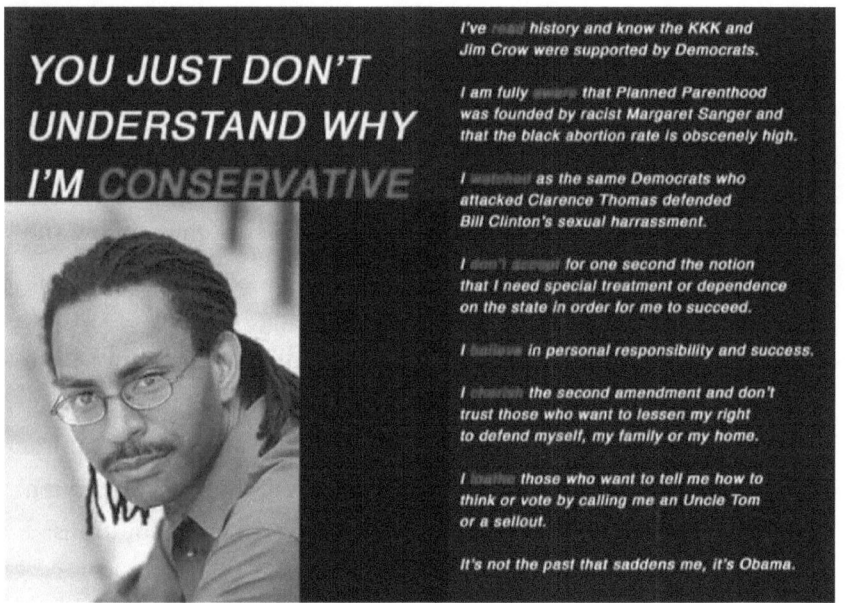

YOU JUST DON'T UNDERSTAND WHY I'M CONSERVATIVE

I've read history and know the KKK and Jim Crow were supported by Democrats.

I am fully aware that Planned Parenthood was founded by racist Margaret Sanger and that the black abortion rate is obscenely high.

I watched as the same Democrats who attacked Clarence Thomas defended Bill Clinton's sexual harrassment.

I don't accept for one second the notion that I need special treatment or dependence on the state in order for me to succeed.

I believe in personal responsibility and success.

I cherish the second amendment and don't trust those who want to lessen my right to defend myself, my family or my home.

I loathe those who want to tell me how to think or vote by calling me an Uncle Tom or a sellout.

It's not the past that saddens me, it's Obama.

PREVIEW FOR COMMANDER-IN-FAILURE

Failure's Prelude

It is called morbid fascination: the mental state you experience when you rubberneck as you drive by a car wreck. It is the reason some folks flock to house fires or show up at murder scenes. It is how a movie like *Faces of Death* becomes a cult hit and spawns six sequels. It is our inability to look away from something we know is terrible. We must look at it, examine it, process it, and understand it.

It is the exact feeling I had on election night 2008. It permeated my heart, mind, and spirit as I walked into the grocery store and watched people pushing their carts with smiles and hope in their eyes. It is a feeling that clung to me like a lingering depression. For a year, it had been a part of my daily makeup as I watched friends, family, and America caught up in the euphoria of Barack Obama's "Hope and Change" and "Yes We Can" election rallies.

I saw history play out in real time. America was going to elect its first black President. Given that the pain of the sixties and the Civil Rights Movement were only forty years removed, it would be a transformative event. The wounds of the past and America's great moral blight were about to be exorcised.

I should have wept like African-American civil rights leader Rev. Jesse Jackson, who unsuccessfully ran for President in 1984. I should have been bursting with hope and pride. Pride as an American, and yes, a deeper pride as a black man.

I felt nothing.

I stood transfixed by the historic moment, yes. But what kept me glued to my television as the election results were announced was my morbid fascination at the train wreck about to hit America.

Why did I feel that way? Barack Obama appeared to be the pinnacle of black achievement in America. Columbia and Harvard educated. Married to one wife, with children. A wife who was not white or a fair-skinned model type—yes, the distinction matters for certain segments of the black community. No hidden side chick popped out during the campaign. Obama was not just well-spoken; he was charismatic and thoughtful, too.

He was a perfect prototype of a man who is black who could be President of the United States.

What else could you want? What more could you ask for?

A lot.

A great deal more than Barack Obama had to offer.

This is not and was not a popular view to take as a black person in America. African-Americans are culturally hardwired to pull for the success of other blacks. Modern-day blacks are freer than at any time in history, but for years we were not seen. Most blacks grew up without images of themselves splashed across the covers of magazines. Before the pouty lips of Hollywood megastar Angelina Jolie were called sexy, they were called big and ugly on black women. We did not see ourselves sprinkled on every television show as the likeable or real smart character like gay characters enjoy as a matter of course... *The Cosby Show* was revolutionary not because it showed a life blacks did not have—there were good, loving, black professional families who flowed in money, it's just that we had never seen them on television.

In sports, we dominated the NFL, except in the quarterback position. Until Tiger Woods, golf was a white man's sport as far as blacks were concerned. Tennis was not far behind. I could go on and on, but the point is that when you are not seen or feel like you have not been seen, you root for the person who looks like you when they show up.

As a black person in America, even if you consider yourself conservative, a part of you automatically roots for other blacks. We see Tiger Woods, and without caring about golf, we want him to win. When Venus and Serena Williams hit the court, you root for them and sit down to take in the only tennis match you may watch all year. You want to see two black women succeed in a sport few blacks have played professionally.

We could be talking about sports, a TV show character, a businessman, a politician—it does not matter. If it is a place or position that many blacks don't occupy, you root for them. When an African-American is the first black in anything, we want them to succeed. We take their side. Their success is emotionally our success.

There are many orthodoxies within the black community that I have rejected. There are good reasons for this, and many will be discussed in this book. But I am not immune to this impulse to side with a black person who has broken the color barrier. When Venus and Serena began playing professionally, they became my favorites partly because they were black. That they were excellent and exciting players helped justify my enthusiasm. But if they had not been amazing on the court, I would have still pulled for them. Ditto for Tiger Woods on the golf course. And in college, it felt good to hear people talk about Colin Powell as a possible future President.

So, with all that said, in a world of accomplishments, in a world full of firsts, there is nothing higher than the idea of a black President. Nothing.

N-O-T-H-I-N-G!

When you are by default rooting for the black person in any walk of life, the idea of not rooting for one who is running for US President is blasphemy and inconceivable to many other blacks. Like garbled computer code, it does not calculate.

So, what was wrong with my mental programming?

Why had I endured the stares of family and friends during Obama's two-year campaign for President whenever I said anything negative about him? Why did I put up with being called a traitor, coon, Uncle Tom, brainwashed, and my personal favorite, being told, "You hate yourself? You hate being black?"

I would like to give you an erudite answer steeped in some mind-altering point of view, but I cannot. I could make a case about the philosophical differences between a Democrat and the beliefs I hold dear that make me a conservative, but that is not the reason I never bought into the hype. My reason was a simple requirement I used on all candidates for President.

The presidency is called the *executive* branch because the President is, in effect, the CEO of the country. He cannot dictate decisions like a king. A President has the House and Senate he must work with, just like a Fortune 500 CEO has a board he must work with. The President, however, does set the direction. He is in charge.

Every President *must* have executive experience. They need to have overseen something: a city, a state, a large corporation or nonprofit, a military division. Something where the buck starts and stops with them, because a President's decisions have consequences, simply because they said yes or no. Before they take on the highest office in the land, they must bring to the job a deep understanding of the type of power they are about to wield. That only comes through a prior deep leadership experience.

America's most successful Presidents have all had that in their backgrounds. They have mostly been former governors, but sometimes they were military leaders. Obama was none of these things.

Obama announced his candidacy for President on February 10, 2007, less than two years after becoming a senator for Illinois. By contrast, Hillary Clinton had been a senator for nearly six years. Before becoming a senator, Obama had served as a state-level senator in the Illinois state house, and before that, he was a part-time professor and full-time community organizer.

Race, sex, and political affiliation aside, what in that list of job titles qualifies anyone to be President of the United States? Obama had barely shown up in the Senate before telling the world he was ready to be President.

Obama was not qualified for the job.

I do not say that as political hyperbole. It has nothing to do with the ridiculous idea that he was born in Kenya. He was not, and it would not make a difference if he had been. His mother is American, and therefore he is American. End of discussion.

I am talking about his resume. He had not been a senator for even TWO YEARS before announcing his intention to run for the highest office in the land. This is like getting a job as a retail clerk at Walmart, getting promoted to store manager, and then a year and a half later telling the investors who hold Walmart stock that the best person to run the company is you. It defies logic.

Here's another example: If I need a brain surgeon and your degree is in law, even if it's from an Ivy League school, you cannot help me. If you are a brain surgeon and I need help with beating charges for a crime I did not commit; you are of no use to me.

The importance of executive experience is that when you are in charge, stuff must get done. Governors can, will, and do argue with their opposition, but as executives, they must balance their budget, maintain the state infrastructure, and handle a hundred other pressing matters. They do not have the luxury of arguing endlessly. They must make sure stuff runs well. That prepares you for being President. Being a senator for five minutes does not.

Considering this, you may be wondering where I come down on the matter of our new President, Donald Trump, who had no political experience prior to running for office. In fact, you're probably burning to know the answer. Well, I will answer this question . . . later in the book, because it is not about President Trump, it is about Obama's eight years in office. But a bit of foreshadowing: Our new President met one of my qualifications for the executive office, though let's just say his run for the post held a morbid fascination as well.

But back to Obama. He simply hadn't amassed the skills necessary for the job he was aiming to get. It gives me no pleasure to say this now or in 2007 when he was running.

I do not hate myself as a black man. No conservative black person does. We want America to succeed, and we are hardwired to want a black person to succeed. When an African-American is one of only a few in any position, and you are black, it is more frustrating and painful to see them fail than it is for a white person. I feel confident in saying that every black conservative in America who has ever spoken against President Obama would have loved—desperately—to see him have the presidency that Ronald Reagan or Bill Clinton achieved.

Yes, President Obama has a high IQ. Yes, he went to good schools. Yes, he appears to be a good father and husband. Yes, he can deliver a rousing and emotionally stirring speech. Iconic words and phrases like "Yes We Can" and "Hope and Change" catapulted him into the Oval Office.

Obama set the world on fire with his campaign. His speeches uplifted most and caused a few to pass out from political ecstasy. On election night, he got 99 percent of the black vote. He got white Republicans to switch and vote for him. He won the popular vote by more than ten million cast ballots. He captured 365 Electoral College votes.

Frankly, he dominated election night.

And for many blacks, he became an instant saint. Before he even stepped into the Oval Office and sat behind the Resolute desk that John F. Kennedy had first worked at in that storied room, they placed him on the same altar as Martin Luther King, Malcolm X, Marcus Garvey, and Nelson Mandela.

So how has Obama worked out for his worshippers?

Are African-Americans better off today than before he took office? Is America in a better place? How are the millions of white Republicans who put him in the office feeling about their vote in 2008? Has America moved into a post-racial time?

If you watch the news, these questions seem absurd. The hope and change Obama espoused did not come to pass. What happened? Obama had a mandate. He had the emotional heart of the nation. Blacks cried the night of his election, and so did many others.

Where did Obama's promise go and why?

It didn't go anywhere. Obama embodied the title of this book: He was a failure.

It's the "why" behind his lack of success that I will attempt to answer in *Failure*. The why provides lessons for future Presidents and leaders. It douses the fire of racial excuses and myths of Republican intransigence. It will tell the tale and do so from the view of Obama's natural constituency.

Obama's singular role in American history is because of his blackness. Make him white, and he would not have been elected

President. His success and failures are different for the black community. The hopes, dreams, and expectations piled onto Obama by others of his race are different. His blackness made and makes being critical of him a cultural grenade.

If you are black, you were supposed to support President Obama. Being critical of him makes you the black sheep in the community—a racial and cultural pariah. Who wants to deal with that?

I certainly did not. But stark reality punched me dead in the face on election night 2008, and the years after have proved the feeling correct. I have no choice but to speak the truth about our first black President.

Our Commander-in-Failure.

Commander-in-Failure Available Now at Amazon.com

www.ingramcontent.com/pod-product-compliance
Lightning Source LLC
Chambersburg PA
CBHW050452290526

45786CB00006B/2265